Tony

Management
Basics

In easy steps is an imprint of In Easy Steps Limited
4 Chapel Court · 42 Holly Walk · Leamington Spa
Warwickshire · United Kingdom · CV32 4YS
www.ineasysteps.com

In Easy Steps Limited supports The Forest Stewardship Council (FSC),
the leading international forest certification organisation. All our titles
that are printed on Greenpeace approved FSC certified paper carry the
FSC logo.

MIX
Paper from
responsible sources
FSC® C020837

Printed and bound in the United Kingdom

ISBN 978-1-84078-427-5

Contents

1 Managing People

What exactly do we mean by management? Different textbooks give different definitions, but people skills – handling staff, colleagues, customers and the boss effectively – are at the heart of good management.

What is Management?

There are many different definitions of management. Many are along the lines of "achieving desired goals through planning, organizing, directing and controlling."

A shorter – and perhaps better – definition is "getting results through other people".

An organization may have an inspiring mission statement, clear goals, a compelling strategy, realistic and challenging work targets, and excellent systems and procedures. But none of these count for much unless it has enthusiastic, committed people. Handling and motivating people is at the heart of effective management.

People skills are the most important attribute of any manager. But they're not enough on their own. The following chapters cover the core management skills needed by anyone operating at any level in any organization. People skills help you to put them all into practice. More advice about team-working and managing teams is given in Chapter 7.

Plain common sense

There are no secrets or magic formulas in this book. Most of it is just obvious common sense. But if you're a conscientious manager, working your socks off in the interests of your organization, you can be so focused on the job in hand and so determined to meet your deadlines, that it's easy to lose sight of some of the basic tools and techniques of effective management.

Most of this book is not about text-book solutions, but about simple, practical things that have been put into practice in the real world and shown to work where it matters – in the workplace.

It's a combination of plain common sense and the kind of unofficial tips that are rarely written down, but which go a long way towards making a decent, effective manager.

Essential Qualities

You don't have to know the latest management theories to be an effective manager. Theories and fashions come and go. Most of the important qualities have been around for years and years, and are likely to endure for many more years:

- Honesty
- Integrity
- Truthfulness
- Industriousness
- Reliability
- Accountability
- Loyalty
- Trustworthiness
- Dedication
- Resilience

And don't forget plain common sense.

Walking the talk

It's not difficult for a manager to lose the respect of colleagues or staff. All (s)he has to do is to tell them one thing, and then to do another himself/herself. For example, make it clear that you expect everyone to be in the office by 9 o'clock on the dot; then roll up yourself at 10. It's pretty obvious that this won't do much for staff morale, but it's surprising how many senior managers don't make the connection.

Being honest and straight

Honesty is important. Don't make promises you won't be able to keep. If you have to pass on bad news, don't shirk the responsibility. Choose the right time and the right way to do it. Do it carefully and sensitively. But do it. Occasionally there may be circumstances which prevent you from telling your people as much as you know yourself. If that is the case, just tell them what you can and stop there. They may not like it, but they will like it even less if you mislead them.

Don't forget

People skills are the most important attribute of any manager.

Don't forget

Remember: deeds always speak much, much louder than words. Setting a good personal example – modeling the behavior and the standards you expect of others – is arguably the most important attribute of any manager.

...cont'd

Don't, whatever you do, express one view of an issue to one person and a different view to someone else. That might be expedient in the short term; but in the long term it will do you no good. You'll be regarded as untrustworthy and duplicitous. On the other hand, the way you express your view, and the facts and arguments you use to support it, may well need to vary according to who you are talking to. You'll want to take account of "where they are coming from." In other words, say the same thing to everyone, but say it differently.

Being fair-minded and even-handed

We're all human, and we all like some people more than others. But a manager won't be fully effective if (s)he is seen to treat some people better than others. Put personal preferences and prejudices aside and deal with your colleagues and staff fairly and even-handedly. If you treat people unfairly you won't get the best out of them.

Avoiding a blame culture

Don't blame people – especially not in public. It's never, ever a good idea to humiliate someone or undermine their self-respect. It's always better to build people up rather than knock them down. A blame culture is unhealthy - and it won't help you to achieve results.

Saying what you think

There may still be a few top managers around who like subordinates who carry out their wishes without question. But most organizations today value managers who think for themselves. Don't be afraid to say what you think – provided, of course, that you have the facts and the arguments to back up your opinion. Once your views have been heard and a decision has been taken, it's your job as a manager to implement that decision, even if you don't like it.

Keeping your cool

Of course, you're allowed to be angry. If someone makes a bad mistake, or fails to carry out an important task, you're going to be very annoyed. That's human nature: it's what you'd expect of any manager who cares about the reputation of his/her unit and its ability to deliver the goods. If something has gone wrong, you need to find out exactly what happened and why – and to do your damnedest to make sure it does not happen again. But all this is best done when you are in a calm, cool frame of mind and you can address the issues clearly and objectively. Losing your temper will not help.

Tools and Techniques

Manage by walking about

Management by walking about (MBWA) is one of the best management tools around. If you're closeted in an office, hunched over a desk or have your eyes glued to a computer screen, you won't see half of what's going on. MBWA is the way to see what's really happening and to find out how people really feel. It also helps your team to see what you're interested in, what your standards are, what you like and what you don't like. You can apply MBWA outside your own team – in other departments and other organizations. Go and see what they are doing! You'll almost certainly learn something.

Beware

A desk is a dangerous place from which to view the world.

Networking

Do all you can to make contacts and to cultivate informal networks: look beneath the surface and you'll find them everywhere – in your own department, in the rest of the organization, and in the outside world. The grapevine often tells you more about what is really going on than anyone will dare tell you openly or officially. If you're faced with a particularly difficult problem, the chances are that someone somewhere else will have come up against something similar. Networking is the way to tap into that kind of informal knowledge and experience. The more networks you are plugged into, the better. Obviously some will be more useful and more reliable than others. Most successful people have an extensive range of personal contacts which they have built up over the years. A good contacts list is worth its weight in gold.

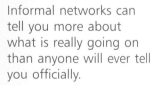

Hot tip

Informal networks can tell you more about what is really going on than anyone will ever tell you officially.

Asking questions – and listening to the answers

Never be afraid to ask questions or to challenge assumptions. The journalist's stock questions are often the best:

- Why?

- When?

- Who?

- Where?

- How?

- What if?

Asking the same question of different people is often a good tactic. You can learn a lot from getting different perspectives on the same issue. Once you have asked the question, listen very carefully to the answer. If that sounds obvious, remember that active listening can be hard work, especially if the person answering goes on a bit!

Avoiding micro-management

The more you can let people manage both themselves and their own work, the better. Don't be afraid to let go. You need to keep an eye on things, of course; to make sure that things are running smoothly and that people are on course to meet their targets. But if you can't see the wood for the trees, you're never going to be an effective manager.

In the middle

In any organization, a manager is in the space somewhere between top management and staff who are carrying out day-to-day tasks. That can be an uncomfortable place to be – especially when ridiculous edicts come down from the top of the organization. You may have to stifle your own reservations (or, at least, not groan too loudly) and persuade your people to accept or do something that everyone – except those at the top – knows is nonsense. But that's your job: you're the manager. You've just got to grin and bear it and get on with it.

14

Being Human

Getting to know them
The better you know someone, the easier it is to get on with them (OK, there might be the odd exception!). Make a real effort to get to know the people you work with. Take an interest in their families and their lives outside the office.   Who knows, you might discover a mutual passion for Renaissance art – or the Bactrian camels of Mongolia! An occasional get-together after work, with an opportunity to talk to people in a less stuffy, more relaxed environment, can be good for building personal relationships – and even for getting to grips with some work-related problem that is too sensitive to discuss in the office.

Being yourself
Don't pretend to be someone you're not. Trying to change your personality to suit what you think the organization wants is almost certainly doomed to failure. The best approach is to understand yourself and your preferred working style(s) as clearly as you can, perhaps using one of the personality profiling models mentioned in Chapter 7. If you really know yourself – how you relate to others, how you deal with information, how you tackle problems – you should be able to adapt your approach to accommodate the needs of those you're working with.

Enjoying work
Enthusiasm can be very infectious. Every job ever invented has its lows as well as its highs. There are bound to be some aspects of your work that are less enjoyable than others – and probably some

that are no fun at all! But being as enthusiastic and upbeat as you can is a good guiding principle. So do all you can to enjoy your work – and help others to enjoy theirs. If you've got a positive attitude, there's a good chance that this will rub off on others, and that they will follow your example.

Beware

If things are going badly, don't take it out on other people.

Taking the job seriously – but not too seriously

You won't be an effective manager if you don't take the job seriously. Meeting your targets, making sure that your team works effectively and efficiently, maintaining high standards, seeking continuous improvement – it's all very important: it's what you're paid for. But it's worth remembering that work is not the be-all and end-all of life. Sometimes the people you're working with will have other things on their mind. Keep a sense of proportion and perspective. Occasionally you'll need to recognize that there are more important things than work.

Sense of humor

Management is a serious business, but the most serious subjects on earth sometimes benefit from a little humor. If you doubt that, listen to any Government debates. Having a sense of humor does not mean cracking jokes. And it definitely does not mean laughing at colleagues or making fun of them. Nor does it mean treating serious issues lightly or flippantly. It simply means recognizing that you don't need to be deadly serious all the time; taking the opportunity now and again to lighten the mood; and being prepared to see the funny side of things.

Don't forget

You don't have to be deadly serious all the time.

...cont'd

Don't be a manager behaving badly

It's easy to be abrupt or offhand or even downright rude towards those around you.

Perhaps you're in a bad mood for some reason – it happens to us all – or you've had some bad news, or you've just had one of those days when absolutely everything has gone wrong.

Or maybe you're just focused on the task in hand, striving to meet a tight deadline, and you resent anything and anyone who breaks your concentration.

Whatever the reason for your bad behavior, just stop and think about the effect on other people. If you're having a bad day, don't take it out on those around you.

Showing passion

If you're passionate about your work and you care – really care - about what you're doing, some of that passion is bound to rub off on those around you.

The chances are it will help them to believe that what they are doing is worthwhile and relevant to the real world, and that it can make a real difference to people's lives.

Influencing and Persuading

Whether you're dealing with your staff, colleagues, customers or your boss, influencing and persuading is an important management skill.

There are usually four key stages:

1 Make sure you thoroughly understand the case you're making: be clear in your own mind about the facts and the arguments.

2 Check that your facts are 100% accurate and make sure that your arguments really stand up.

3 Put yourself in the shoes of those you're seeking to influence or persuade. Try to understand "where they are coming from". That will help you to decide what approach to take and which facts and arguments to use.

4 Put your points across (whether orally or in writing) as clearly and concisely as you can.

Beware

Don't keep your boss in the dark.

Handling the Boss

Keeping the boss informed

Don't try to pull the wool over your boss's eyes, or keep him/her in the dark. If there is bad news, be up-front about it. If you're not, the chances are that, sooner or later, (s)he'll find out about it from someone else anyway. There are few things senior people dislike more than getting a sudden, nasty shock about which they have had no prior warning, even though the unpleasant facts have been known for some time at a lower level in the organization. Don't keep bad news to yourself.

Understanding your boss

Take time to understand your boss. Find out:

- How he or she sees their role;

- What makes him/her tick;

- What his or her real priorities are;

- How he or she spends most of their time;

- What pressure he or she is under;

- Where the pressure comes from;

- What he or she really likes;

- What he or she dislikes;

- What he or she finds really annoying!

His problems: your opportunities

We all have our good points and bad points, our strengths and our weaknesses - even the boss. It's your job to help the boss. If you can make him/her look good, it won't do your relationship any harm. If your own strengths can compensate for some of the boss's weaknesses, that's great: you'll make an excellent team. If your boss has a problem, it's a real opportunity to show how helpful and resourceful you can be. If the boot's on the other foot and you have a problem you need to take to the boss, try not to present it to him/her without suggesting how it can be solved.

Dealing with a difficult boss

No-one is perfect. The chances are, you won't like everything your boss does or agree fully with the way (s)he operates. Whatever kind of boss you have, you've got to survive and to make the best of it. So you might just have to follow Churchill's advice. KBO - keep buggering on!

If life becomes intolerable and your boss is consistently acting in a way which is unfair or unreasonable, you'll have to do something about it. If you don't and you end up totally stressed out, your health is bound to suffer.

Try the following:

1 Make a note of the key points you're going to make.

2 Arm yourself with the chapter and verse of some specific examples.

3 Rehearse both the key points and the specific examples.

4 Try an informal oral approach.

5 If that does not work, put your concerns in writing. Keep it clear, concise and specific. Avoid any biased judgments or comments: be as factual and objective as you can.

If this does not produce a result, it may be time to call for the cavalry: copy your note to your boss's boss. If whatever you are complaining about is happening consistently, (s)he may already have heard about it. Your complaint might confirm existing suspicions and convince him/her of the need to take action. Stranger things have happened.

Don't be afraid of the top team

However senior your colleagues are, remember that they are just fallible human beings like the rest of us. Just like you, they have to get out of bed in the morning, wash, dress, eat, drink, urinate and do everything else human beings do.

If you're meeting the CEO or MD for the first time, try not to be overawed. (S)he won't eat you alive.

Handling Customers

Hot tip

When people talk, listen completely. Most people never listen.

Listen to them

Remember that your customers are people too. In dealing with them, use the same people skills you use when dealing with your colleagues and your staff. Pay attention to what they tell you.

Feedback from those who use what you produce – whether that's a computer program, an investment portfolio or an internal report – is the best way of making sure you are providing what the customer wants. If you always put the customer first, your management decisions are unlikely to go far wrong.

Customers are not all the same

Different customers have different needs. What satisfies one may not satisfy another. Remember that your customers are individuals, with individual likes and dislikes. That may mean adapting the way you and your team work.

Remember that the customer's needs are more important than your own convenience.

Personal Development

Getting a mentor

A mentor is usually a senior colleague, whom you trust and whose advice you respect, who agrees to act as an informal adviser and counselor. Few people can resist responding when their views are sought, and senior managers often find it rewarding to help younger talent.

A good mentor should be able to help with almost anything, from the detailed and trivial to the strategic. The mentor's role is private and confidential.

A personal plan

Instead of making a New Year's resolution, make a career-related resolution.

One well known politician is said to have sketched out his life plan on the back of a cigarette packet while at university. He set out his goals, the last of which saw him arriving as the British Prime Minister at 10, Downing Street. He didn't quite make it, but perhaps it was not such a bad idea. Your goals will be different, but you can apply the same rule. There are three key principles:

1 to set your sights high;

2 have a clear objective to aim at;

3 set yourself a deadline which is challenging but realistic.

It's easy to live only in the here and now. If you're in a busy job, with lots of immediate problems to solve and deadlines to meet, it's all too easy to neglect your own future. A personal plan, setting out where you aim to be in five or ten years' time, and how you hope to get there, can help to keep your managerial career on track.

Keep it to yourself, in case it does not fit with how others see your future.

Hot tip

See Career Development check list on page 170.

Summary

- Handling and motivating people is at the heart of effective management

- People skills enable you to put into practice all the other competences which every manager, operating at any level in any organization, needs

- Pay attention to old-fashioned virtues such as honesty, integrity and accountability

- Walk the talk – model the behaviors and standards you expect of others

- Make a real effort to get to know the people you work with

- Treat everyone fairly and even-handedly

- Network to build up an extensive range of personal contacts

- Ask questions and challenge assumptions

- Don't be afraid to say what you think – but make sure you have the facts and arguments to back up your opinion

- Learn how to influence and persuade

- Remember that your boss's problems are your opportunities

- Map out a personal career plan with a clear objective

2 Managing Time

A manager's time is too expensive to waste. Effective time management is one of the most important management skills.

Why Time Management is Critically Important

Time is limited: it doesn't last for ever. We need to make the best use of it we can – whether we're thinking about the amount of time we have left on earth, how we're going to spend the weekend, or how we use our time at work.

The need to control or reduce costs is a fact of corporate life, and staff salaries are often the biggest single cost. Cost-cutting, perhaps involving an increased use of technology and a flatter management structure, can mean fewer people doing more work. Salary costs have to be balanced against each person's contribution to the organization.

Effective time management requires:

1 A clear focus on the results you're seeking to achieve;

2 Resistance to distractions and irrelevancies which get in the way and don't help you to achieve your objectives;

3 Control of each day's agenda so that you make the best possible use of the time available.

Beware

Don't waste time surfing the net or constantly checking your email inbox.

Wasting time

It's easy to waste time: there are so many ways. Reading stuff we don't need to read. Constantly checking our email in-box. Surfing the net to check up on the football results or the winning lottery numbers. Going to meetings we don't need to go to. Phoning or texting our friends. Chatting to colleagues about things we don't really need to discuss.

Spending time on inconsequential stuff because it's easier than tackling the difficult task we should really be getting to grips with. I could go on…

The 80:20 rule

The Pareto Principle

Pareto was an Italian economist who lived in the early 1900s. He observed that about 20% of the people controlled or owned 80% of the country's wealth. In the 1940s a quality management pioneer working in the United States, Dr Joseph Juran, realized that the same principle was applicable to almost any aspect of management.

Let me explain this with a couple of examples. On a production line, 20% of product defects typically cause 80% of the problems; and 80% of a company's revenue typically comes from sales made by 20% of the sales force.

Importantly for any manager, focusing on just 20% of the work is likely to produce 80% of the results. The trick, therefore, is to identify, and spend most of your effort on, that critical 20%. If you're able to do that, the chances are you'll see a big improvement in your effectiveness.

Hot tip

Remember the 80:20 rule.

Concentrate on the vital 20%

So spend most of your time, your energy and your creative thinking dealing with that vital 20% of your work that will probably account for 80% of your outcomes.

This should mean focusing on those work objectives and targets that are most important to your organization, to your boss and (last but not least) to your own career prospects. It means doing the big things well.

Prioritizing

Is it urgent or important?

If you're faced with a new task, ask yourself two simple questions:

1 Is it urgent?

2 Is it important?

If it's both urgent and important, do it as soon as you can. If it's urgent but not important, get one of your team to do it. If it's important but not urgent, you can do it later. If it's neither urgent nor important, don't do it!

Being clear about priorities

The trouble is, you may have several tasks in front of you that are both urgent and important. So you need to prioritize your priorities, and that's not always easy.

During recent management training seminars in two Central European countries, officials in both told me that it was impossible to rank their priorities. "Everything is a priority," they said, quite sincerely. "But if everything is a priority," I pointed out, "what that really means is that nothing is a priority."

If you have lots of important tasks on your plate, ranking these in order of priority can be difficult and painful. You may need to think very carefully about the criteria you use. It's not an easy process, but it really is necessary.

Keeping priorities under review

It's important to review your priorities regularly. The world does not stand still. Remember that you're operating in a constantly changing environment. Work objectives and priorities cannot be set in stone. What was a top priority at the beginning of the year may become less important a few months – or even a few days - later, for all kinds of reasons. There may be changes in the political or economic environment or in your organization's policies or personnel. There may be new developments or an unforeseen crisis which has to be dealt with.

Make sure that your priorities reflect the current reality.

Lists and Deadlines

The "to do" list

It's a good idea to begin each day by jotting down a list of things you aim to get through, and the order in which you'll tackle them. For some of them you might even want to go a stage further and write down not just the tasks themselves (e.g. chair staff meeting), but also the outcome you hope to achieve (e.g. persuade them that the CEO is not such a bad guy).

Inevitably, your plan will sometimes be thrown out of kilter by an unforeseen emergency or by a boss who believes that his/her deadlines are more important than yours; but that's life.

Hot tip

Get into the habit of setting deadlines – both for yourself and for others.

Hot tip

See Simple "To Do" list on page 171.

Setting deadlines

Get into the habit of setting deadlines – both for yourself and for others. If you have several tasks to do, write down the date by which you'll aim to complete each one. The date needs to be realistic but reasonably challenging.

If it's too generous you may find yourself falling prey to Parkinson's Law: "Work expands so as to fill the time available for its completion." A deadline concentrates the mind. Without a copy deadline, Management in easy steps would not have been written.

Controlling Work

Don't be too reactive

Don't be too reactive to the demands of others. You yourself must decide how you spend your time. Be clear about what it is you have to do, and make sure you're in the driving seat.

Remember that your boss will judge you on the work you produce and the results you achieve. So concentrate, first and foremost, on meeting your own objectives and targets.

If you're the kind of person who likes to be helpful to colleagues (and most of us are), discipline yourself to put your own interests first. By all means be helpful to others, but resist any requests which get in the way of your own priorities.

Don't go to every meeting

For some managers, meetings are a way of life. They may even enjoy them, perhaps seeing them as a far pleasanter way of spending time than getting to grips with the pile of difficult stuff they should really be tackling. Even the most conscientious manager may welcome the excuse to have a break away from the desk.

Remember that you don't need to go to every meeting to which you are invited. Attending meetings can become a (bad) habit and take up an enormous chunk of your time.

If you're asked to go to a meeting, ask yourself whether or not it will help you to achieve your own work objectives. If it won't – and unless there is some other objective reason which justifies your attendance – don't go.

Beware

Don't be too reactive to the demands of others.

Beware

Don't go to meetings that don't help you to achieve your own job objectives.

Hide yourself away

If you're faced with a particularly tricky task, mark off a time-slot in your diary when you won't be available to others. Find somewhere quiet away from colleagues where you won't be disturbed, such as a meeting room that's not being used.

Or you may be able to work at home, or in a quiet corner of your favorite café or bar.

And give yourself an incentive. Resolve that you won't leave (or have lunch or go to bed) until you have completed the task.

Take a break

However busy you are, it's not a good idea to slog away at your desk for hour after hour without a break. If you do that, the quality of your work is bound to suffer.

If you have to grab a sandwich at your desk for lunch, at least get out of the office for half an hour to stretch your legs and get some fresh air.

Handling Paper

Handle each piece of paper only once: be D A F T

It's easy to waste time by having to reread a paper you read a few days ago without deciding what to do with it. Try to handle each piece of paper only once. There are really only four ways of dealing with it:

1 **D**elegate it

2 **A**ct on it yourself

3 **F**ile it away for future reference

4 **T**hrow it away

If you need to take action on it yourself, try to do it straight away.

Occasionally you may get an important paper which you do really need to look at carefully, but cannot deal with immediately. You might be doing something that's even more urgent and important. In that case, it's sensible to put it aside until you have the time to look at it properly. But if you do that, make sure you read it and deal with it as soon as you possibly can. The next time a paper lands on your desk, remember **D A F T.**

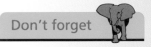

Handle each piece of paper only once.

Beware

Don't read stuff you don't need to read.

Don't read everything

Despite IT and wishful thinking about the paperless office, the chances are that your organization and those it deals with produce lots of paper.

Don't feel obliged to read every piece of paper that lands on your desk. A glance at the heading will often be enough to tell you that it can go straight into the wastepaper basket.

And even if you need to look at it, you can probably skim through without reading every word.

Look out for key headings:

- Summary

- Conclusions

- Recommendations

- Action points

You're probably quite discriminating when it comes to your leisure reading. Apply the same kind of self-discipline to the stuff you read at work.

Only read what will help you to do your job or develop your career.

Punctuality and Energy

Being on time

It doesn't matter whether you're meeting a VIP or having a routine meeting with your team. Make a habit of being on time. If you're late, you're implicitly telling people that your time is more important than theirs. Value other people's time as much as your own.

If you're chairing a meeting, begin on time and don't wait for anyone who is late. If you do, you're wasting not only your time but that of everyone who has made the effort to be punctual.

Senior people who habitually keep others waiting may believe that this enhances their own importance. All it does is show a lack of consideration for others. Of course, an unforeseen crisis can prevent anyone from being on time, but that should be the exception.

Energy can get you to the top

Those who make it to the top of any organization are usually intelligent individuals with good communication skills and a clear focus on results. But there is something else that is at least as important – sheer energy.

Look at any sphere of activity – sport, politics, the arts, the media, business – and you'll see that those who reach the very top often have no more talent or intelligence than their peers. What sets them apart, more often than not, is sheer energy and drive. Energy can take you a long way.

Summary

- Focus on the vital 20% of your work that will probably account for 80% of your outcomes

- Do the big things well

- Faced with a new task, ask yourself: Is it urgent? Is it important?

- Set deadlines both for yourself and for others. Make sure they're challenging but realistic

- Write a daily "to do" list

- Prioritize your priorities

- Don't be too reactive – spend most of your time on meeting your own objectives

- Don't read everything, and don't go to every meeting

- Handle each piece of paper only once

- Faced with a tricky task, find a quiet place and a time when you won't be available to others

- Be punctual

- Energy and drive can get you to the top

3 Managing Presentations

Making a presentation is a great opportunity to make an impact. Preparation is the key.

Hot tip

Making a presentation is a great opportunity to make an impact. Don't waste it.

Hot tip

See Presentation check list on page 172.

Preparation

If you're not used to it, it can be a nerve-racking experience: having to stand up in front of a group of people and make a presentation. It's natural to have a few butterflies - especially if you have just moved into a new job or you are faced with a large or an unfamiliar audience.

It's important to do your homework: the better prepared you are, the more confident you'll feel. Make sure you're clear about the purpose of the presentation and the expectations of the audience. Get to grips thoroughly with the subject-matter, and give careful thought both to the content and to the structure of what you're going to say.

Preparation is the key: if you're well prepared, you'll find it easier to relax and to be yourself. Try to approach the task in a positive frame of mind. The truth is that the audience will want you to do well. You have something useful to say and they want to hear it. They haven't come along to catch you out! Don't think defensively or imagine that you need to have every conceivable fact and figure at your fingertips. Just focus on the essentials and on putting those across as clearly as you can.

Making a presentation can be a great opportunity to get known and to make an impact on people. Make the most of it. Believe it or not – if you have prepared thoroughly and you know exactly why you're making the presentation and what you want to achieve – you may find yourself looking forward to it.

Rehearse

A rehearsal is the only way to time a presentation accurately, and it is usually time well spent. Don't imagine that a short presentation does not need rehearsing: this can be harder to give, and can require more careful preparation, than a long talk.

There are three ways to rehearse a presentation:

1. into a dictating machine

2. in front of a mirror

3. in front of a colleague or friend or partner who is prepared to give constructive feedback

The Audience

Before you begin preparing your presentation, take time to think about the audience. If you don't already know them, you'll need to do some research.

You need to ask the following questions:

- Who are they?

- Where are they from?

- How many of them are there?

- Why are they attending?

- How much experience do they have?

- What is their interest likely to be?

- How much do they already know about the subject?

- What will they want to know?

- What are their expectations?

- What do they want to get out of it?

You need answers to all these questions before you begin to think about the content of your presentation.

Talk to them beforehand

Most people feel more relaxed when they are talking to people they know. So a presentation to a small group of colleagues you work closely with and know quite well is likely to be less stressful than a presentation to a large room full of strangers. It always helps if there are a few familiar faces in the audience. If you're giving a presentation to a group of people you don't know, it's a good idea to chat to a few of them beforehand if you get the opportunity. Sometimes this can give you a last-minute clue about what the audience are hoping to get out of the presentation. More importantly, exchanging an informal word or two with a few people before you begin can transform an impersonal mass of humanity into real human beings with individual feelings and foibles. You'll probably find that they are easier to talk to, and more receptive to hearing what you're going to say, than you had imagined.

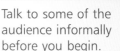
Hot tip

Talk to some of the audience informally before you begin.

The Purpose

Why are you making the presentation?

It may sound obvious, but it's important to be crystal clear about the purpose of your presentation. There are many possible reasons:

- to pass on information

- to report on something that's happened

- to explain a new initiative or policy

- to seek to persuade the audience to a particular point of view

- to urge the audience to take action of some kind

Whatever your reason for making the presentation, the important thing is to be clear about it.

Aims and objectives

Get your aims and objectives down on paper. Write yourself a one-sentence explanation of why you're making the presentation and what you're seeking to achieve: a few specific aims and objectives, framed – and this is important – from the audience's perspective. For example, a presentation about a new staff assessment system might have the following audience-based aims:

1 to have a clear understanding of the rationale for the new system

2 to be able to explain to staff the key principles and the main stages in the annual assessment process, and

3 to be able to apply the new system with effect from (say) 1 January

The Venue

Hot tip

Check out the venue
beforehand.

Think about the setting

Next, think about the setting for your presentation.

- Will you be addressing half a dozen colleagues in your office?

- Or two hundred people in a conference room?

- Or something in between?

In planning your presentation you'll need to take account of the environment in which you'll be working.

- If you're not already familiar with the room, it's worthwhile (especially if it's a big occasion) checking it out in advance if you possibly can.

- Look at the seating arrangements and try out the sight-lines.

- If you're going to be using visual aids, check what equipment is available and make sure you know how to operate it.

Fumbling around in front of your audience searching for the right control switch is unprofessional, wastes time and damages your credibility.

The Method

Think about how you can get your message across most effectively. At one extreme, you may decide to speak informally, perhaps eschewing all technical aids and simply using a few notes (or even just key words) to remind yourself of the ground you need to cover. At the other end of the spectrum, you might have to make a formal speech to a large audience – in which case you'll probably need to write it all out in full, and to read it out, either from a copy on the lectern in front of you or from an autocue. Most presentations fall somewhere between these two extremes.

Don't read it out

With the sole exception of a formal speech to a large audience, it's never a good idea to read a presentation. If you are constantly looking down at your script, it's very difficult to maintain eye contact with the audience. Moreover, reading out a prepared text word for word can give the impression (albeit unfairly) that you lack confidence or don't know the subject as well as you should. And, since we don't speak in the same way as we write, it can also make the speaker seem stilted and insincere. It's very much better to prepare speaking notes and to use those to remind yourself of the points you're going to make.

Using what works best for you

There are three main ways of preparing speaking notes:

1 Write headlines or key points on a sheet of paper

2 Use cue cards, again with headlines or key points

3 Write structured notes: these can include not only headlines or key points, but also essential facts and figures, arguments, examples and anecdotes

Each method has its pros and cons. Writing just headlines or key points allows for natural delivery, flexibility and interaction with the audience. If you use this method you'll need to be very familiar with the subject-matter. This applies also to cue cards, which can be held easily in the hands and are therefore useful if you're going to be standing or moving around.

The main disadvantage of both these methods is the risk that you won't have all the details you need. But you can expand your headlines or key points to include a few "memory joggers" – perhaps to remind you of specific examples or anecdotes you're going to use.

Structured notes enable you to have more information to hand. One refinement of this method is to use a highlighter pen to differentiate the material that's essential from that which is merely desirable. Then, if you are running short of time, it will be easy for you to skip all the non-essential stuff.

With trial and error you'll discover which method works best for you.

Visual Aids

People take in information much more readily through their eyes than through their ears. If you listen to a lecture, the chances are that you'll remember one or two bits of what you're told, but you'll forget a great deal of it. However, if you see a visual image – whether it's an object, a drawing, a photograph, a video clip or a PowerPoint presentation – you're more likely to remember it. One picture can be worth a thousand words, and visual aids can help to arouse and maintain interest. They won't always be useful or appropriate, but they can often help to get the message across.

Flip charts and whiteboards

If your presentation is short, informal, addressed to just a few people, and deals with a subject that is pretty straightforward, a PowerPoint presentation probably won't be appropriate. You might nevertheless want to reinforce or illustrate one or two key points, and in these circumstances a flip chart or a whiteboard can be very useful. If you prepare it beforehand you won't have to waste time, and to turn your back on the audience, during the presentation itself. Make sure that your handwriting is legible, and that it can be read by those at the back of the room. A flipchart is ideal for small groups – and, of course, it's particularly useful for capturing ideas and suggestions from the audience and for brainstorming sessions.

Beware

Limit the number of Powerpoint slides and the amount of text on each slide.

PowerPoint

PowerPoint can be a very effective and powerful tool, but it needs to be used carefully and correctly. Two key points to remember:

1 limit the number of slides

2 limit the number of words on each slide

As a very rough guide, allow two or three minutes per slide. So if you're making a 20-minute presentation, you probably won't need more than about eight slides. And don't put too much information on each slide: a heading and five spaced-out bullet points, each with no more than six words of text, is ideal. Don't be tempted to read from the screen, and remember to switch the machine off when it's not being used: a glaring white light distracts the audience.

Powerpoint or talk book?

Don't think of PowerPoint as the automatic choice for any presentation. It is often over-used. If your presentation includes charts, maps, images or other graphical material, PowerPoint will probably be appropriate. If, however, you are speaking to a small audience and your material consists mainly of words, a talk book may be more effective. You can give each person a copy of the book and simply talk them through the key points.

Video

A short video extract can sometimes be useful – for example, to add emotional impact to a message, or to illustrate a complex process; but if you're not careful it can become a barrier between the speaker and the audience. Use sparingly – only in short sequences and only to explain or illustrate specific points.

Plan B

Whatever method of presentation you choose, it's always sensible to have an alternative up your sleeve – a Plan B – just in case, for example, the PowerPoint equipment does not work or the promised flip-chart fails to materialize. Don't risk getting caught out by hiccups of this kind – it's embarrassing and unprofessional. The simplest plan B is often to come along armed with prepared notes which will enable you to stand up on your hind legs and talk to the audience.

Content

Content obviously depends upon the purpose and the subject-matter of the presentation.

One common mistake is to cover too much ground and to give the audience more detail than they can absorb. It's important to think really carefully about the key points and the essential information you need to get across. Put yourself in the audience's shoes, and cut out anything they're likely to find irrelevant or uninteresting.

For many presentations, it's good practice to concentrate on putting across a small number of key messages as clearly and concisely as you can.

Beware

Don't try to cover too much ground or to make too many points.

Repetition

Any politician knows that repetition can be a good way of ramming home any message. If you've got three key points to get across, you might want to mention them briefly in your introduction, to explain and elaborate on them in the main part of your presentation and, finally, to reiterate them in your conclusion.

But don't overdo the repetition, or you'll risk sending the audience to sleep. If you're saying essentially the same thing three times over, it's best to do it in slightly different ways and to use different words.

Specific examples and anecdotes

In the main part of your presentation you'll need to explain and elaborate on your key points. You'll need to give facts and figures, but it's very important to reinforce and illustrate these with specific examples or anecdotes. These add human interest and bring any presentation to life. And they are much more likely to be remembered than dry statistics. The best, most memorable presentations usually make extensive use of anecdotes and specific examples.

Questions

Many speakers are at their best when answering question - they come across more naturally and convincingly. So don't be afraid to invite questions. Make it clear at the outset whether you're prepared to take them during the presentation or only at the end. Then deal with them honestly and thoughtfully. Be brief and to the point. If you don't know the answer, say so: don't waffle or guess. If the question is unclear, make sure that you and the rest of the audience understand it. This can often be done by paraphrasing it back to the speaker.

If you're unlucky enough to be faced with someone who is difficult or obstreperous, just be firm and polite.

Don't forget

Invite questions, and answer them crisply and honestly.

44

Making an Impact

Beginning and ending

For any presentation, the audience's attention is at a peak at the beginning, when they're imagining (perhaps optimistically!) that they're about to hear a brilliant speaker giving a stimulating talk on a riveting subject. After the first minute or two, interest will begin to flag. People will perk up again at the end, when you've signaled that you're about to finish and they're looking forward to the coffee break or the lunch. So take particular care about how you begin and how you end your presentation. That's when you have the best chance to make a strong personal impact.

Begin with a remark that draws the audience in and makes it easy for them to relate to you and to what you're about to say. Don't try to be a stand-up comedian. Humor is a funny (peculiar), quite personal thing. Something that strikes you as hilarious might fall as flat as a pancake. Just explain, in no more than a couple of sentences, what you're going to be talking about and how it relates to their particular needs. And then make your key points: no more than three or four – that's as many as most people will remember. If you can do all that within the first five minutes, there's a good chance that you'll have grabbed their attention.

Illustrating your key points with personal anecdotes and specific examples adds human interest and helps the audience to remember them. This is really important.

When you're near the end, say something to make it clear that you're about to finish (e.g. "before we adjourn for coffee…"; "in conclusion…"; "before I sit down, let me just…"). With any luck, that signal will make people sit up and take notice of your concluding remarks. Try to end on a strong, positive note.

Hot tip

Be yourself – don't put on an act.

Beware

Don't try to be a stand-up comedian.

Don't forget

End on an upbeat note.

Eye contact

Eye contact is important. A presentation is a form of communication, and communication is a two-way process. Eye contact enables you to check that the information you are giving is being received. If people are yawning or staring at the ceiling, it's a fair bet that you are not exactly grabbing their attention.

Don't just concentrate on one person or on one part of the audience. Look around, towards the back of the room and in the middle as well as at the front row. Try to spend a few seconds looking at different people in different parts of the room. This helps to draw people in and shows that you are speaking to the whole audience.

Length

Twenty minutes should be long enough for almost any presentation. That's about as much as most audiences can take. The attention span of most people is surprisingly short. On average it tails off after about eight minutes. After that, they begin to lose interest or switch off entirely. Introducing variety – a visual aid, an anecdote, or a question to the audience – can help to maintain interest. But if you see closed eye-lids or just bored, vacant expressions, you'll know that it's time to sit down.

Speed and voice projection

If you're slightly nervous, or if you feel you have a lot of ground to cover and not much time in which to cover it, you might find yourself speaking rather quickly. Almost certainly, this will make it difficult for the audience to follow and take in what you are saying. So make a conscious effort to slow down. Project your voice, vary the tone, emphasize key words and phrases, and speak a little more slowly than normal. If you can do that, your words will gain added weight and authority.

Being yourself

Don't try to take on an alien persona for the benefit of your audience. You're not an actor. Pretending to be someone you're not just does not work. Be as natural as you can and let your own personality come through. Whatever that is, it's sure to go down much better with the audience than any attempt to be someone else.

Bad Presentations

- Speaker goes on too long
- Poor delivery (e.g. reads it out, no eye contact, monotone)
- No real grasp of subject-matter
- Content is not related to the audience's specific needs
- Packs in too much information
- Confused or illogical structure
- Too much or too little detail
- No opportunity to comment or ask questions
- Bad use of visual aids (e.g. slides with too much text)
- Equipment problems
- Unconvincing body language
- Inappropriate jokes or humor
- Inappropriate dress
- Lacking energy and conviction
- Responds to questions by waffling
- Makes questioner look foolish
- Loses thread of argument
- Overweening or arrogant attitude
- Superficial treatment of issues
- Tells audience only what they already know

Summary

- Prepare thoroughly

- Take time to focus on the audience

- Be clear about the purpose of the presentation

- Set yourself some audience-based objectives

- Have a rehearsal

- Consider visual aids

- Don't read the presentation – use speaking notes

- Twenty minutes should be long enough

- Begin by drawing the audience in and making it easy for them to relate to you and to what you're about to say

- Use specific examples and anecdotes

- Take questions – and deal with them honestly

- End on a strong, positive note

4 Managing Meetings

Meetings can be useful for doing all kinds of things. They can also be a complete waste of time. They don't have to be long and boring.

Preparation

Bad meetings

During a career stretching over forty years I have attended hundreds of meetings. Many of them were a complete waste of time. They dragged on and on, and were often excruciatingly boring. People arrived late or they came unprepared – sometimes because they had not had proper notice or an agenda; sometimes because they had not made the time to read the relevant papers. Sometimes they did not arrive at all. Participants were allowed to ramble. Sometimes one or two people dominated the entire meeting. The person in the chair lost control – or never had control – and occasionally even he (or she) did not seem to know what the meeting was all about and why it was being held. There were no conclusions and meetings ended without anyone having the faintest idea what would happen next.

Do we need a meeting?

If you work an 8-hour day and you have two hour-long meetings every day, that's a quarter of your working life spent in meetings. Over a 40-year career that adds up to more than 20,000 hours of meetings. That's more than two years of your life! OK, that might be an exaggeration: you'll probably get a few meeting-free weeks. It's still a hell of a lot.

Meetings can be very useful, but they can also be a complete waste of time. Quite often there are more effective and more efficient ways of dealing with things.

It's very easy to have a bad meeting - one which leaves the participants feeling frustrated, resentful of the time they have wasted, and unclear about the outcome. We have all attended meetings like that. If you want to have a good meeting, there are three simple rules:

1. Make sure that you really do need to have the meeting – that it's the best way of dealing with the matter

2. Be crystal clear about the purpose - what you're seeking to achieve

3. Prepare thoroughly

Hot tip

Ask yourself: do I really need to have this meeting?

What's the purpose?

The first essential of any meeting is to be clear – and to make sure that others are clear – about the purpose. Why are you having a meeting?

There are many possible reasons:

- to pass on or obtain information

- to seek views

- to identify possible ways of dealing with a problem

- to take a decision

- to get people to take action

- to persuade people to support a particular point of view

- to resolve differences of opinion

- to review progress on some project

- to plan future work

Whatever the reason, the first imperative is to be clear about why you're having the meeting.

OK, you're clear about the purpose. Before you push ahead with the arrangements, just spare a moment or two to double-check that a meeting really is the best way of dealing with the matter. Could it be dealt with more effectively and more efficiently by some other means? Perhaps by sending out an email? Or making a few phone calls? Or even popping round to have a chat, face to face, with the key people involved?

Make sure you really do need a meeting.

Hot tip

Make sure everyone understands the purpose of the meeting.

First steps

Once you're quite sure that you need to have a meeting and you're crystal clear about the purpose, you can begin your preparation. So you need to:

1 Identify the key people – those whose presence is essential

2 Think about others with an interest who ought to be invited

3 Fix the date, time and venue

4 Consider what background papers or other information participants will need to have before the meeting

5 Consider what outcome you hope to achieve

6 Consider whether you should prepare the ground beforehand by speaking to any of the key people

Hot tip

Circulate the agenda and papers in good time.

Circulating papers

It's important that those who are attending the meeting receive the agenda and any reports or other papers they need in plenty of time.

Above all, avoid giving participants the papers only when they arrive at the meeting – it wastes time and reduces your chances of having an effective meeting. The participants will spend all their time reading the papers instead of listening and contributing to the discussion. And if the papers contain a lot of new information on which you're seeking comments, people may decline to express a view until they have had an opportunity to study the detail. You can hardly blame them.

Length

Most meetings go on too long. It's good practice to set a firm time-limit at the outset. The optimum length obviously depends upon the amount and complexity of the business to be discussed.

But for many meetings 30 minutes or an hour is an adequate and realistic timeframe.

If there is an agenda with several items of business, it's often useful to designate a time-limit for each item. Put the most urgent and important items near the top of the agenda – just in case, despite your best efforts, you do not succeed in getting through the whole agenda in the time available.

If an exceptionally long meeting is unavoidable, make sure there are periodic comfort or coffee breaks. These will allow people to check messages or make a quick phone call.

It can be a good tactic to schedule a meeting for late in the day, when people are keen to get off home. There will be less danger of irrelevant digressions and inconsequential interventions. Anyone who tries to hijack the meeting and go off at a tangent on some old hobby-horse will not be very popular.

Most people won't want the meeting to overrun, and won't mind if it finishes earlier than expected. The deadline of the train they want to catch will concentrate their minds wonderfully. You'll have a much better chance of getting contributions that are crisp and to the point.

Hot tip

Meetings don't have to be long and boring.

53

Logistics

Participants can easily get hacked off if the organization goes awry. Little hiccups can have a disproportionate effect on the mood of any meeting. If people are irritated they are less likely to make a constructive contribution. So make sure that everything runs like clockwork.

1 Make sure the room is suitable for the type of meeting you're having

2 Check, or get someone else to check, the seating arrangements

3 Make sure that any technical equipment needed is in place and is working properly

4 Make sure everyone knows when and where the meeting is being held and how to get there

5 If people are coming from outside the building, make sure the reception and security people know who to expect, and that any necessary passes have been organized

6 Lay on tea and coffee (or at least water) and notepaper

It's all very basic stuff, but if any one of these little things is overlooked, it can jeopardize the entire meeting. I've seen it happen!

Distractions

Don't let people use mobile phones during the meeting: it's impolite and unprofessional, and will irritate other participants. Use of laptops, Blackberrys and PDAs (personal data assistants) is becoming increasingly common. Encourage anyone who uses these during the meeting to do so with consideration for other participants.

Opening and Closing the Meeting

Making participants feel comfortable

People are more likely to make a constructive contribution if they feel at ease. So it's worth taking the trouble not only to introduce yourself to any participants you don't know, but also to make everyone feel welcome and, in particular, to introduce any newcomer(s). It's always a good idea for the person in the chair to arrive a few minutes early so that (s)he can exchange an informal word or two with people before the meeting begins. Even if these exchanges are just about the weather or the latest football or baseball match, they can help to break the ice and set the scene for a friendly, constructive discussion.

Introduction

It's vital to get the meeting off to a good start. The opening comments from the chair are critically important. (S)he needs to:

1 welcome participants and make them feel comfortable

2 set the tone – show that the meeting will be conducted in a businesslike manner

3 demonstrate that (s)he has a grasp of the subject matter

4 explain the purpose of the meeting and make sure that everyone understands what (s)he is expected to contribute

5 explain the ground rules – the timeframe, handling of the agenda, how questions will be dealt with, and so on

Don't forget

For action points, specify who will do what and by when.

Conclusion

The chair's concluding remarks are what people will be left with, and it's vital to get them right. The precise content obviously depends on the type of meeting, on how successful it has been, and on the outcome. But at virtually any meeting the person in the chair should:

1 summarize the main points of the discussion

2 take especial care to identify any conclusions reached, recommendations agreed or decisions taken

3 go over any agreed action points, making clear exactly what action has to be taken, by whom, and by when

4 set out any next steps (such as another meeting!)

5 thank participants for their attendance and end on an upbeat, positive note

Chairing Skills

Politeness and firmness

Chairing a meeting is an excellent opportunity to demonstrate your interpersonal skills. You need to treat participants with courtesy and consideration. But you also need to be firm and businesslike.

You may need to shut some people up, and to encourage others to open their mouths. It's important to make sure that the meeting is not dominated by one or two opinionated characters who like the sound of their own voices. Sometimes the quietest people have the best ideas. You need to keep the meeting on track, and to discourage over-long or irrelevant interventions.

You need to make sure that everyone has an opportunity to express their views; but it's best to avoid embarrassing people or putting them on the spot, because that is more likely to result in a negative, defensive reaction than a positive, constructive contribution.

Summarizing, clarifying, questioning

One of the most important chairing skills is the ability to make sense of rambling and incomprehensible contributions. Summarizing a long and boring intervention in two or three crisp sentences helps everyone to follow the discussion – and to stay awake.

To summarize what someone has said you need to

1. make a brief note of the key points

2. regurgitate these using clear, simple language

If someone uses terms or jargon that won't be understood by others, ask them to spell it out in language people will understand. The same goes for those who lose themselves in technicalities or complex, over-long sentences.

If something is said which is not clear, it's the chair's job to clarify it. This can often be done by asking the speaker to repeat what has been said, or by rehearsing it back using simpler language ("If I understand you correctly, what you're saying is…"). And if someone makes a dubious statement or assertion, don't hesitate to interrupt and ask for some supporting evidence.

Summarize, clarify and question: if you're in the chair, that's your job.

Pushing your own point of view

Sometimes you will have formed your own view, beforehand, of the conclusion you want the meeting to come to or the decision you want it to take.

- Take care not to alienate participants by pushing your own view too strongly. It's often good tactics to save your own comments until others have had an opportunity to speak.

- Getting someone else (either a member of your own team or another participant) to articulate a strongly held view of your own can be an effective way of getting your point across without making people feel that you are taking unfair advantage of your role in the chair.

Note-taking

It's essential to have an accurate note of the meeting. If you don't record what has been agreed and who is to take what follow-up action, it will be difficult to chase people up if they do not do what has been agreed.

Nominate someone to take a note. The more familiar (s)he is with the subject matter, the easier (s)he will find it to follow and make sense of the discussion. So if it's a subject new to the note-taker, (s)he should be encouraged to prepare by reading the relevant papers. The note-taker needs to have a good seating position (it's often best to be next to the person who is in the chair) with a clear view of all the participants.

Note-taking tips

However senior you are, you'll probably find yourself acting as note-taker yourself at some meetings. It's impossible to write as quickly as you can speak. So it's not a good idea to attempt a verbatim record. Instead, just concentrate on capturing the key points.

Here are two simple tips for note-taking:

1. Develop your own personal shorthand - not Pitman's, just a rough and ready way of getting things down on paper as quickly as you can. You can often do this by abbreviating words, omitting vowels or just writing initials. As long as you yourself know what the shortened word or initials stand for, that's all that matters. A variation on the same theme, which will appeal to some more than others, is to use the kind of abbreviations and language that's used in text messaging.

2. Watch out for key words and signals. If someone says "I'm going to make three main points" or "to sum up…" the note-taker should be on red alert. It's especially important to watch out for – and to record clearly and accurately – key points, conclusions, decisions, recommendations and action points.

Styles of notes and minutes

The style of note required will depend on the type of meeting. Sometimes the note-taker will have to adhere to a prescribed format (one that is always used in the organization for that type of meeting), but sometimes (s)he may have to decide what style to use. There are three main options:

1. Action points: for an informal meeting with your own team (perhaps to discuss an ongoing project or a forthcoming event) a simple list of action points may well be sufficient. List each action point, if necessary adding a sentence to describe exactly what will be done, and against it put the name of the person responsible and the deadline. So you know who will do what and by when.

2. Detailed record: at the other end of the spectrum, for a large, formal meeting or conference (at which, perhaps, senior representatives of different organizations are discussing a major issue) a detailed record, attributing comments to individual speakers, may be appropriate.

3. Summary record: many meetings fall somewhere between these two extremes, and for these a summary record is often the best option. This summarizes the main points made during the discussion (usually without attributing these to individuals), and sets out, as appropriate, the conclusion(s) reached, recommendation(s) made, decision(s) taken, and action points agreed.

Housekeeping points

Whichever style of record is used, it should include details of

- when and where the meeting was held

- who chaired it

- who attended

- which organizations or departments they represented

It's important to record the names and contact details (telephone numbers and email addresses) of all participants (one way of collating these is to get people to inscribe them on a piece of paper circulated during the meeting).

This will make it easy if, after the meeting, the note-taker needs to obtain clarification of something that was said, seek additional information, or chase up action points.

Beware

Little hiccups over logistics and practicalities can have a disproportionate effect on the mood of participants.

Participating Effectively

Preparation

It's not only the person in the chair who needs to prepare. Anyone participating in a meeting needs to prepare if they are to make a useful contribution. You'll need to read the relevant papers and get to grips with the subject matter. If this is difficult or contentious you'll probably need to sound out the views of others in advance of the meeting. You'll need to be clear about what you want to get out of the meeting. Then you can plan your contribution and write yourself a brief speaking note.

Listening

If the business is so important or so difficult to deal with that a long meeting is inescapable, both the person chairing the meeting and the other participants will need to make a conscious effort to maintain concentration.

Listening is hard work. Absorbing information and getting to grips with the key points requires a conscious effort, especially if the speaker just drones on and on, without making much effort to interest the listeners. It's very easy to let your attention wander; to think about more interesting things, such as the novel you're reading or the holiday you're planning.

Put all those pleasant thoughts to the back of your mind. Look at whoever is speaking and concentrate on what (s)he is saying. It might be boring, but it's what you're being paid to do.

Tips

Here are some key tips for contributing effectively to meetings:

- read the papers and get to grips with the subject matter

- be clear about your objective

- write yourself a brief speaking note

- secure a good seating position

- look alert and ready to contribute

- maintain eye contact

- speak with energy and conviction – and not too fast

- build on others' contributions

- label your interventions ("I would like to make two points…")

- speak clearly and succinctly

- be positive and constructive (if you have to say "no" to something, suggest an alternative to which you might be able to say "yes")

- generate light, not heat - stay calm and don't lose your temper

- take your own notes of key comments/points (even when there is an official note-taker)

Bad meetings

- No clear purpose

- Go on too long

- No agenda or papers

- Chair has no real grasp of subject-matter

- Chair has no control

- Chair is domineering or insensitive

- Dominated by one or two people

- Attended by the wrong people

- Poor logistics (e.g. room, seating, heating/ventilation, refreshments, technical aids, interruptions, etc)

- Nothing agreed – no clear outcome

- Nobody knows what will happen next

Summary

- Make sure you need to have a meeting

- Be crystal clear about the purpose

- Prepare thoroughly, and get the papers out in good time

- Make sure the logistics run like clockwork

- Use opening remarks to welcome participants, explain the purpose, set a businesslike tone, demonstrate a grasp of the subject matter, and explain the ground rules

- Be polite but firm

- Use interpersonal skills to encourage contributions and to discourage over-long or irrelevant contributions

- It's the chair's job to clarify, question and summarize

- Use closing remarks to: summarize the main points; identify conclusions, recommendations and decisions; go over action points (who will do what and by when); and set out any next steps

- Try to end the meeting on an upbeat, positive note

- Make sure you have an accurate record

- If you're participating, have a clear objective and write yourself a brief speaking note

5 Managing Projects

Today any manager, at any level in any type of organization (public or private sector), is likely to have to manage a project of some kind.

Definition and Purpose

Don't forget

A project must have a clear purpose, a specified timescale and dedicated resources.

The need to manage projects effectively is nothing new - think, for example, of the some of the massive civil engineering works undertaken in the nineteenth century. However, project management as a recognized, distinctive discipline dates from around the mid-1950s. Initially used for major construction, infrastructure, energy and communications projects, its use has spread to virtually every type of activity.

Project management has become a subject studied in centers of learning all over the world. It has given rise to an enormous body of literature and countless methodologies, many of them seemingly impenetrable to anyone who has not been to a top business school.

Yet there's really nothing difficult about project management. In fact, it's very simple. It boils down to three important things:

1. Being clear about the end-result – the outcome you're seeking to achieve

2. Identifying the steps you need to take, and putting mechanisms in place, to achieve that outcome

3. Ensuring that these steps are taken, so that the project is completed on time, within budget and to the required standard

Almost anyone can become a competent project manager.

How to define a project

Projects come in all shapes and sizes, from organizing a media event (perhaps to launch a new product or announce a new initiative) to developing a multi-million pound computer network.

Most definitions of a project have two key characteristics:

- a clearly defined timescale within which it must be completed

- clearly defined resources with which to carry it out

Being clear about the purpose

The first essential thing is to be crystal clear about the purpose of your project.

What is the outcome you are seeking to achieve?

- Has it been defined by your boss or your top management team?

- Do you need to define it for yourself?

Think about the project's added value and the difference it will make to the organization.

Define the desired outcome as clearly and precisely as you can.

Stakeholders

Getting buy-in

Any major project needs to be supported by the key stakeholders. This is critically important. If you don't have their support, the chances are that, sooner or later, you'll hit trouble. So take care to identify the key people. Cast your net as widely as you can, both within your organization and beyond, and make a list of them.

Then go down the list and annotate it from two different perspectives:

1 how much power or influence the stakeholder has in relation to the project

2 how much interest (s)he has in it

This will enable you to put each stakeholder into one of four categories:

1 if they have a lot of power and a lot of interest in the project, try to **involve** them

2 if they have a lot of power but not much interest in the project, **keep them informed** about it

3 if they have a lot of interest in the project but little or no power, **listen** to them

4 if they have neither power nor interest in the project, you can probably **ignore** them

Hot tip

Get the key stakeholders on board at an early stage.

Hot tip

See Stakeholder Analysis worksheet on page 173.

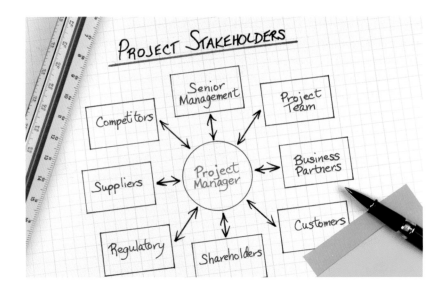

Periodic reviewing of stakeholders

Stakeholders change. Some will disappear from your radar screen and new ones will appear. And, for a whole range of reasons, the amount of power they have, or the amount of interest they have in your project, may change over time. So it's important to keep an eye on them, especially in the case of a major project taking months or years to complete. Periodically review your list of stakeholders and the extent to which you need to involve or inform them. From time to time you'll need to make some changes.

Keeping key stakeholders in the picture

There are plenty of reasons why it's a good idea to keep your key stakeholders involved or informed – especially in the case of a major project with far-reaching implications.

- it helps to gain their commitment and cooperation

- it helps to guard against unrealistic expectations

- it gives them an improved understanding of the issues and problems involved in implementing the project

- it can help to avoid unpleasant surprises – both for the stakeholders and for the project manager

Risks and Obstacles

Hot tip

See Risk Register
worksheet on page 174.

Identifying the risks and the obstacles

Once you're clear about the purpose of the project and the desired outcome, and you have identified your key stakeholders, the next step is to think about all the things that could go wrong. If it's a big project, there will be lots of them; but even if your project is the production of a simple report or a sales leaflet, there are bound to be some things that could prevent its successful completion.

You need to identify the risks and potential obstacles. Brainstorming (see Chapter 9) can be a useful technique for this.

Probability and impact

Once you have identified all the risks and obstacles, you need to ask, in respect of each one, two important questions:

1 How probable is it that this will materialize?

2 If it does materialize, what will the impact be?

If something would have a huge impact on the project (say, an earthquake) but is extremely improbable, you can ignore it. Equally, if something is very probable (say, a member of your team leaving to take up a new job), but would have little or no impact on the project, that too can be ignored.

Ranking the risks and obstacles

A simple and easy way of ranking both for probability and for impact is to give each risk and obstacle one of five rankings:

Hot tip

See Risk Profile
worksheet on page 175.

- Very high

- High

- Medium

- Low

- Very low

If you then put this information onto a graph or spreadsheet you'll be able to see at a glance the probability and the impact of each risk and obstacle.

Now you can focus your attention on those which are most probable and will have most impact on the project. For example, you might decide to concentrate just on those which come out with at least a high ranking both for probability and for impact.

Dealing with risks and obstacles

Once you have identified those things likely to materialize which will have a significant impact, you need to decide what, if anything, you can do about them. There are four main possibilities:

Don't forget

Every project has risks – make sure you know how you'll handle those which are most likely to arise and would have a significant impact.

1 **prevention:** action to stop the risk arising or to remove the obstacle

2 **reduction:** action to reduce the probability or to limit the impact

3 **contingency:** action that can be taken if the risk or obstacle does materialize

4 **acceptance:** simply accept that no action is feasible

In an extreme case, where significant risks or obstacles which will have a high impact on the project are very likely to materialize, and where nothing can be done about these, it may be necessary to abort the project.

In practice it is almost always possible to find some way of at least reducing the probability or limiting the impact.

Outputs and Outcomes

Breaking the project down into manageable chunks

By now you're not only clear about the project's desired outcome. You also know who the stakeholders are, what risks and obstacles you face, and how you're going to handle these.

The next step is to break the project down into manageable chunks of work. You can approach this task from two angles: what you put into the project, and what you get out of it. It's usually best to begin by defining what you want to get out of the project – the outputs.

Terminology

It's easy to be confused by some of the terminology used in project management. Words such as aims, goals and objectives can also cause confusion, not least because management gurus tend to define these in slightly different ways.

The **aim** or **goal** is the end-result you want to achieve. So both these words are really just alternatives for **outcome**. An **objective** is usually something intermediate which you need to achieve in order to end up with your desired outcome.

Some organizations use these terms differently – for example, thinking of outputs as activities, or having targets (rather than outputs) for absolutely everything. Others limit targets to a small number of key outputs: a manager may have, say, a dozen outputs which (s)he is responsible for delivering. But if two or three of these outputs are critical to the organization's success, these may be expressed as specific, quantifiable targets which (s)he is expected to hit (or to exceed) within a specified timescale.

It's best not to get too hung up on any one definition of any of these words. What's important is to understand the (essentially simple) steps and processes involved.

Let's call the end-result you're seeking to achieve the outcome, and the specific things or products that the project will deliver the outputs. It's essential to ensure that the outputs we identify really do contribute to the desired outcome.

Hot tip

Don't worry too much about the terminology used in project management. The important thing is to understand the – relatively simple and straightforward – steps and processes involved.

Make sure your outputs are SMART

- Specific
- Measurable
- Achievable*
- Relevant*
- Time-limited

Hot tip

Outputs need to be SMART.

Specific

Each output needs to be specific. It must be defined as precisely as possible. It must specify exactly what is to be accomplished and by whom.

Measurable

Each output must be quantifiable: it should be possible to put specific figures against it, so that what has been achieved can be measured. This is easier with some things (for example, sales or production) than it is with others, but even with 'softer' outputs (such as personal development) it should be possible, with careful thought, to put some measures in place.

Achievable

Outputs need to be challenging, but it's vital that they are achievable. If they are impossibly difficult to achieve, that will discourage and demotivate people. And that's the last thing you want. So make sure you have realistic, achievable outputs.

Relevant

Each output needs to be relevant to the end-result (i.e. the outcome) that you are seeking to achieve. Sometimes it may be tempting to establish certain outputs simply because they are easy to measure; but that's counter-productive. Each output must contribute to achieving the desired outcome.

Time-limited

It's essential to establish a time limit for each output. Clear deadlines help to keep the work on track and to prevent drift.

Some versions of this model use 'agreed' rather than 'achievable' and 'realistic' rather than 'relevant'. In this case, 'agreed' means agreed with key stakeholders.

Planning and Implementation

Plan your project

These are the steps you can take to plan your project:

1 Be clear about the end-result (the outcome) you are seeking to achieve.

2 Define the specific outputs (and/or targets) that will enable you to achieve that desired outcome.

3 Agree the timeframe.

4 Clarify what resources (human and financial) are available.

5 Draw up a list of the activities that need to be undertaken in order to produce each of the specified outputs. Think carefully about linkages and dependencies - the order in which activities are carried out. Some can be carried out in parallel, whereas some will be dependent upon the completion of other activities. It's good practice to assign responsibility for each activity to one named individual.

6 Establish milestones so that you can monitor progress.

S pecific
M easurable
A chievable
R elevant
T ime-based

Using a Gantt chart to plan your activities

A Gantt chart is a horizontal bar chart widely used in project management to plan, coordinate and track specific tasks. It was originally developed in 1917 by Henry L. Gantt, an American engineer and social scientist, as a production control tool.

A Gantt chart is useful for planning activities over a period of time.

Here is a very simple example. Obviously, the timeframe and the units of time allocated to each activity depend on the nature and the complexity of the project.

	January	February	March	April	May
Activity A	▓				
Activity B		▓			
Activity C	▓	▓			
Activity D			▓	▓	
Activity E					▓

Beware

Some of the methodologies used in project management can appear complex, but most of the techniques involved are simple and easy to understand.

75

Hot tip

See Gantt Chart worksheet on page 176.

Milestones and performance criteria

How do you know whether or not you're on track to complete your project on time, within budget and to the required standard? The answer is to establish performance criteria and milestones – specific points throughout the implementation period when you will monitor how things are going.

For each milestone, specify exactly how much progress should have been made (e.g. outputs, budget utilization, performance criteria to be met). It's important to establish performance criteria which are relevant and appropriate for whatever it is that you are seeking to measure. They may include such things as statistical comparisons, quality checks, regular reports and audits.

Once you've established milestones and performance criteria, you'll be in a position to compare actual performance with planned performance. You'll know whether or not you're on schedule. If you are, fine. If you're behind schedule, consider what action you can take to get the project back on track. If you're ahead of schedule (it can happen!), go out and celebrate.

Project management software

Software programs (such as Microsoft Project) can be useful to help plan and monitor a project. These typically include Gantt charts and some of the other tools mentioned in this chapter. Some people like these programs and some don't, but it's worthwhile taking a look at what is available.

Being on time

Many projects are time-critical. If your project includes the launch of a new product at a conference scheduled for 1 March, you won't be popular if your publicity material for the launch is not ready until 2 March.

If being excellent means being late, it is usually better to be a little less excellent but to be on time.

Putting it all into practice

You're now equipped to put all this stuff into practice.

- You're clear about the desired outcome and the outputs you have to deliver in order to achieve it

- You know who your stakeholders are, what the likely risks and obstacles are, and how you'll handle them

- You know how much time you have and what resources are available

- You know what needs to be done and who is going to do it

You have everything you need to be a brilliant project manager.

Don't forget

Being on time is often more important than being perfect.

Summary

- Be clear about the purpose and the desired outcome of your project

- Identify and categorize stakeholders

- Involve key stakeholders – those who have both a lot of power and a lot of interest in the project

- Identify risks and obstacles

- Consider what action you can take to deal with any risks or obstacles that materialize

- Break the project down into manageable chunks of work

- Establish outputs which are specific, measurable, achievable, relevant and time-limited

- Agree the timeframe and the resources available

- Plan the activities that need to be undertaken in order to achieve each output

- Assign responsibility for each activity to a named individual

- Establish milestones and performance criteria to enable you to keep track of progress

- Make sure you complete the project on time, within budget and to the required standard

6 Managing Communication

Problems within any organization can often be traced back to a breakdown in communication. Successful organizations recognize this and make effective communication a key priority. Every manager needs communication skills, and the more senior you are, the more important they become.

Hot tip

Clarity and brevity are the essentials of effective communication.

Ways of Communicating

The communication revolution

In recent years no other aspect of management has changed as rapidly and radically as communication. Twenty five years ago most letters, reports, minutes and memos were either dictated or written out in longhand. Then they were typed up.

New technology has transformed the way we communicate. Personal computers, emails and the internet have revolutionized our working lives. Now it's almost impossible to imagine how we managed to work without laptop computers and cell phones.

Today these are essential management tools, but soon they too will be replaced by a new generation of electronic gadgets.

Choosing how to communicate

How you communicate will be affected to some extent by the culture of your organization – "the way things are done around here" – as well as by your own personal style.

But most of all, it should be dictated by the particular circumstances

- what you have to communicate

- how important it is

- who you have to communicate it to

You have to use your experience and your common sense.

If you have something to pass on to your team or your colleagues – whether it's a piece of information, an instruction or some advice – it's worthwhile taking a few seconds to think about how you're going to do it. There are usually several options:

- call a meeting

- send out an email

- send out a memo (either as hard copy or as an attachment to an email)

- telephone

- cascade (pass it on to one other person, say your deputy, and ask him/her to pass it to the rest of the team)

- one-to-one (either at your desk or by visiting them at their desks).

There are lots of possibilities. Decide which is the most appropriate and effective way to communicate that particular piece of information.

If you decide to communicate something that's important orally one-to-one, either face-to-face or on the telephone, it's a good idea to keep a brief note. You'll be surprised how useful this can turn out to be.

Energy and confidence
If what you have to communicate is important, it's usually best to do it with energy and enthusiasm. Diffidence or hesitancy can undermine the most brilliant message.

On the other hand, even a weak message can convince if it's put across with energy, conviction and confidence.

Understand the Message

Hot tip

Make sure you thoroughly understand whatever message you're communicating.

You can't communicate effectively if you don't understand – really understand – the message you're seeking to put across. It's a good principle to never, ever, write or say anything you yourself do not understand. If you're asked to explain something you've communicated and you can't, you'll look foolish and it will undermine your credibility.

So the first, crucial step is to make sure that you understand whatever it is you're communicating.

1 Take time to brief yourself thoroughly

2 This might involve looking at previous papers or files, or talking to a colleague or a specialist who knows more about it than you do

3 If the subject is very important or very complex you might even need to do a little research

It's vital to get to grips with the subject and to make sure that you've got the essential facts at your fingertips. Whatever the subject matter, whatever the audience, you won't be listened to with respect unless you can show that you know what you're talking about.

Understand the Audience

Put yourself in their shoes

Once you're sure that you thoroughly understand the message you're communicating, the next step is to make sure that you understand the audience. This can be simple or it can be difficult.

- If you're communicating with colleagues you know well, that's one thing

- If your communication is going to colleagues you don't know well or to people outside your own organization, you may need to do a bit of research to find out how they're likely to react

The key here is to put yourself in the shoes of the person or the organization you're communicating with. Think about how much they already know about the subject and how much interest they have in it. Consider what concerns they will have and how they are likely to react. This will give you some clues about how you can put the message across most effectively.

Tell the truth

It's important to give everyone the same message – even if it's likely to be unpalatable to some people. If you give different people a different message, you'll get a reputation for unreliability and double-dealing. It might enable you to deal more easily with the immediate issue, but it will damage your credibility and do you no good in the long run. So don't change or twist the message – keep it the same for everyone.

...But tell it differently

On the other hand, it's sensible to adjust the way you put the message across – the facts and the arguments you use to support it – in order to make it as acceptable as you can to the individual or the organization you're dealing with.

- Make sure the essential message is the same, but tweak the way you deliver it

- Just choose those facts and arguments that are most relevant and are most likely to go down well

Of course, the better you know your target audience – the more you understand "where they are coming from" – the easier this is.

Hot tip

Put yourself in the shoes of the audience.

Don't forget

Keep your message consistent.

Beware

Don't waffle and beat about the bush. If you speak at great length without saying anything much, people will soon lose interest and switch off.

Tactics

The tactics you use to put across the message most effectively depend both on the audience and the subject matter. Sometimes it's best to come right out with a succinct statement of your conclusion, and then to back this up with the facts and the arguments.

Sometimes – especially if others are unlikely to agree with your opinion or your conclusion – it is better to take your audience by the hand and lead up, step by step, to the conclusion. Use whichever tactics are most appropriate and most likely to succeed, bearing in mind both the subject matter and the person(s) you're communicating with.

A two-way process

Communication is not just about giving out information. If you're communicating orally, you need to give those you're communicating with an opportunity to react. This helps to ensure that the message has been received and understood. It's important to give people an opportunity to express their views and to ask questions. Whether the reaction is positive or negative (or something in between), you need this feedback.

With written communication, too, it's usually a good idea to make it easy for the recipient(s) to provide feedback. You can often do this simply by including your contact details, such as an email address.

Don't forget

Listen as well as tell.

Communicate Clearly and Concisely

Keeping it short and simple (KISS)

If you want to communicate effectively, clarity and brevity are essential.

Ask the first person you meet in a strange town for directions, or listen to any radio chat show, and you'll realize that many people have difficulty expressing themselves simply and clearly. Whether you are communicating orally or in writing, keep it as short and simple as you can. That way, it will have more impact and be easier to remember.

KISS (Keep It Short and Simple) is the easiest of acronyms to remember. The longer and more complex the message, the less likely it is to be remembered. Politicians and public relations people know this. That's why, day in, day out, they use catchy slogans and short, snappy sound-bites. They know it works.

Written communication

As a general principle, write in a style that's as close as you can make it to the way you speak. That doesn't mean using slang or colloquialisms that would look ugly on a printed page. It just means using plain English: direct, everyday language.

The English language has two main derivations, Latin and Anglo-Saxon. Usually the word derived from Anglo-Saxon is shorter (and often more concrete) than the Latinate equivalent – for example, begin, rather than commence; end, rather than terminate; light, rather than illuminate. If there is a short word that will do the job, choose that in preference to a longer alternative.

Use short sentences. They are easier to read than longer sentences with complicated constructions and lots of subsidiary clauses. Between 15 and 20 words is a good average.

Finally, use short paragraphs. A page of solid text, or one page split into just two huge paragraphs, does not invite you to read it. Short paragraphs are easier on the eye.

Hot tip

KISS – keep it short and simple.

Hot tip

Use plain English and short words.

Long versus short words

Ascertain	find out
Assist	help
Commence	begin
Component	part
Concept	idea
Concerning	about
Demonstrate	show
Discontinue	stop, end
Endeavor	try, attempt
Establish	set up, form
Forward	send
Illuminate	light
Initiate	start
Necessitate	require, need
Permit	let
Principal	main
Provide	give
Purchase	buy
Regarding	about
Terminate	end

Avoiding jargon

All organizations use jargon, and that's fine – provided everyone involved understands it. But if you're communicating with the outside world, it's vital to avoid jargon, acronyms and, indeed, any terms with which the recipient is unfamiliar. You need to make sure that every word you use is comprehensible. If you use jargon to communicate with the outside world, you might just as well use a foreign language.

Presentation

Written communication also needs to be clearly presented.

1. Use plenty of white space – decent margins and paragraph breaks

2. Use headings and sub-headings in bold to make it easy for readers to find their way through

3. Take care over the font type and size, making sure that it's appropriate for the purpose and easy to read

4. If you have a small number of key points to put across, use bullets to make them stand out

Checking and proof-reading

However much care you take over the text, it's very easy to make simple mistakes or typos. Once you have sent it out, it's too late to do anything about it. If the text has gone out with some ghastly mistake and you have to issue a subsequent correction, that won't do your professional reputation any good at all.

1. Check the text meticulously before you send it out. Look especially carefully at names (people can get very annoyed if you misspell them), initials denoting titles or academic qualifications, and numbers. These are all things it's very easy to slip up on.

...cont'd

2 It's also a good idea to get a colleague to cast an eye over it. If you are very close to a subject it is sometimes difficult to spot errors: you might read what is in your mind rather than what is on the page. A colleague who is less closely involved with the substance of the communication may pick up typos or other little mistakes that you have missed.

Put it away for a day

When you have finished writing anything, it's always a good idea to put it away for a day or so and then to look at it again with fresh eyes. As a writer I know that the final text is always better than the first draft. If you put it away and come back to it later, you'll be able to look at it more objectively.

Invariably you'll spot something you can improve:

- perhaps a sentence you don't need

- a word that's not quite the right one

- something important that you've omitted

- something that can be said more clearly and more concisely

Give it a try: it really does work.

Obviously, when you're up against a tight deadline, this may not be possible. If that's the case, at least get a member of your team to cast an eye over it before you send it out.

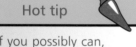

Hot tip

If you possibly can, put any written communication away for a day and then look at it again.

Emails, Websites and the Internet

Emails

Emails are wonderful. With a few taps on the keyboard you can send your message anywhere in the world. It's quick and easy. It enables you to send out all kinds of documents without going to the trouble and expense of printing and posting out hard copies.

Whatever business your organization is in, emails are an indispensable aid to handling the work effectively and efficiently.

Take as much care over an email as you would over a letter or any other more formal communication.

1 Make sure your spelling is correct and that you address people professionally

2 Don't use slang or sloppy language

3 Check the text carefully and take a few moments to reflect before you send it out – especially if you're angry or you're reacting to something about which you feel strongly

Once it's gone out, it's too late to change. So make sure that the text is accurate and businesslike.

Because emails are so quick and easy to send and to receive, there's a tendency to over-use them. Sometimes, because of the nature of the document or its confidentiality, a hard copy really is essential. And sometimes nothing but a one-to-one conversation, either on the phone or face to face, will do.

So before you hit the send button, just take a moment or two to consider whether an email really is the best option.

Don't forget

Take as much care over emails as you would over any more formal communication.

Beware

Don't bombard people with communications they don't need to have.

Don't forget

Before you hit the send button, take a second or two to check the text and to consider whether an email is the best option.

...Don't let them rule your life

It's very easy to waste time constantly checking your inbox or reading and responding to inconsequential emails that are much easier to deal with than the piece of work you should really be tackling. It's a good idea to reserve one or two specific time slots during the day for dealing with emails, perhaps first thing in the morning and last thing in the evening. If an email needs a reply, try to send it the same day.

Don't let emails rule your life. Use them, like any other business tool, to help you do your job.

Websites and the internet

Website design and use of the world-wide web are outside the scope of this book. It's worth noting, however, that a well-designed website, which both customers and the public at large can find their way around quickly and easily, is something which no organization can now afford to be without.

Thanks to the internet it's possible to obtain instant information about anything under the sun. But some information sources are more reliable than others, and not everything you read on a website is true. So take care and use the internet sensibly. And don't overuse it: it's easy to waste an enormous amount of time surfing the net and looking at all kinds of stuff that's absolutely fascinating – but not at all relevant to the job you are being paid to do.

Don't forget

Avoid words or jargon the recipient is unlikely to understand.

Management speak

All too often written communication both within and between organizations is bedeviled by "management speak." Words like strategy and coordination are sometimes used simply because the writer thinks those are the sort of words he's expected to use. They don't always have much meaning.

Phrases like "You will wish to be aware…" and "happy to discuss" do not always mean precisely what they say. They may be euphemisms for something the writer does not want to spell out explicitly.

Is this what they really mean?!

Ball park figure – a figure that has as much chance of being accurate as I have of winning the national lottery.

Blue skies thinking – I'll contribute some theoretical, totally impractical ideas. I'm much too important to worry about the detail.

Coordination – a means of either duplicating or counteracting what others elsewhere in the organization are doing.

For information – don't even think about commenting on this. But if it goes wrong, I won't forget that you knew all about it.

Happy to discuss – there's a lot more going on here than meets the eye. I haven't told you the half of it.

In due course – in a very long time (if I remember).

I'd welcome your thoughts – I haven't the foggiest notion what this is about. Can you help me out? Then I can pinch your ideas and take all the credit.

I have taken careful note of your suggestion – your suggestion was rubbish and it's gone straight into the waste paper basket.

I hope this is helpful – I know very well that this is not at all helpful. Please go away and don't bother me again.

Review – something is going wrong, but we can't admit it.

Stakeholders – all those people who know nothing about the organization and care even less.

Strategy – a word which makes people think you know which direction the organization is going in, when neither you nor anyone else has a clue.

Target audience – the poor souls who have to put up with all the nonsense the organization puts out.

Work/life balance – I'm the boss here and I'm going home early. You can stay behind and work late.

You will recall – I didn't either until I dug out the old papers.

Summary

- Problems within any organization can often be traced back to a breakdown in communication

- Whenever there is something you need to communicate, think carefully about the most effective way of doing it

- Be clear about the message you're communicating

- Put yourself in the shoes of the person(s) you're communicating with

- Put the message across as clearly as you can.

- Keep it short and simple (KISS)

- Tell the truth, and give everyone the same message

- Adjust the way you put the message across to make it as acceptable as possible

- Communication is a two-way process: you need to listen as well as tell

- In written communication use: plain language; short words, sentences and paragraphs; headings, sub-headings and bullets

- Check and proof-read the text carefully, and then put it away for a day or so and look at it again with fresh eyes

- Use emails and the internet sensibly

7 Managing Teams

A team is more than a bunch of people who work together.

Why a Team?

The days of autocratic bosses and employees who just do as they are told are pretty much over. No organization can hope to survive today unless it makes the best possible use of its human resources. That means using the:

- experience
- knowledge
- skills

of all its people.

Every one of them has individual

- strengths
- weaknesses

Team-working is the way to make the most of them.

An effective team adds value because it contributes more than the sum of its individual components.

Definition of a Team

What is a team?

Let's begin by defining what we mean by a team. There's no one definition accepted by all the experts, but most agree that the essential characteristics include:

- a clearly defined membership

- a role which is understood and accepted throughout the organization

- clear aims and objectives

- continuous collaboration and interdependency

- team goals which individuals alone could not achieve

We can turn this into a one-sentence working definition:

"a group of people, with complementary skills, experience and roles, who work together to achieve common and agreed aims."

Team Development

Putting a team together

Occasionally you may find yourself in the happy position of setting up a team from scratch. You'll probably find that resources are limited and that you'll have to settle for less than you would ideally like.

Putting a team together can be exciting: you'll probably need to use all your interpersonal skills to get them all on board.

Making the best of what you've got

More often, you'll have to work with the team you're given. Your job as a manager is to make the best possible use of the resources you've got. That means using the individual skills and knowledge of each member of your team to maximum effect.

Stages of team development

Probably the most widely accepted model of team development is B W Tuckman's (published in Psychological Bulletin in 1965).

He saw team development in four stages:

1. **forming:** members of the team come together, get to know one another, explore their strengths and weaknesses, and win each other's respect

2. **storming:** attitudinal and temperamental differences emerge and are discussed and debated

3. **norming:** the team settles down and works out ways of working effectively together

4. **performing:** the team, having dealt with its internal problems, gets stuck into its work and achieves its goals

Team Leadership

Definition of leadership

What do we mean by leadership? As with management, there are lots of different definitions. To my mind one of the best is "getting people to do something because they want to". It's probably easier, however, to identify what we expect of a leader. For my money a leader needs:

- to have vision

- to give purpose and direction

- to lead by example – "walk the talk"

- to inspire and motivate – to get the best out of people

- to involve people in matters that affect them before final decisions are taken

- to think strategically and set clear objectives

- to seek continuous improvement

- to home in on key principles and issues

- to act honestly and even-handedly

- to be visible and approachable

- to communicate clearly and persuasively

- to have energy and enthusiasm

- to be resilient and tough under pressure

Leading by example

If you're the team leader, the very best way to lead is by example: "walk the talk". You need to model, and to put into practice on a daily basis, those standards which you are seeking to instill into others.

Setting a good example is such an obvious principle of leadership that it should hardly need saying. Yet during a management career of some 40 years I have known one or two very senior people for whom the proverb "do as I say, not as I do" might have been invented.

Hot tip

Delegate to make optimum use of each individual's skills and experience.

Knowing what works for whom

We're all different: the way we work, the way we think, the way we relate to those around us, the way we respond to praise or criticism, the way we cope with the unexpected. Some people respond well to pressure, and thrive when faced with a challenging deadline. Others need lashings of praise and encouragement if they are to produce their best work. Yet others need a firm framework, and respond better to a stick than a carrot.

What works for one may not work for another. Remember that your team is a collection of individuals, all with different personalities, different strengths and weaknesses - and different foibles. As their manager, it's your job to get to know what makes each of them tick.

Delegation

Delegation (dealt with in more detail in Chapter 11) enables you to make maximum use of your resources. It also helps the team to gain new experience and new skills, and to grow and develop. There are both immediate and longer term benefits.

I have led different teams in different parts of the world doing very different types of work. The contexts and the culture - and the personalities of team members – could hardly have been more different, but in all of them delegation enabled me to make effective use of whatever skills and knowledge each individual had.

If you decide to delegate a piece of work, don't just give it to whoever happens to be passing by. Give the matter a little thought.

- Think about what that task will involve and what skills will be needed.

- If it's urgent you'll need to pass it to whoever has the time, the skills and the experience to do it quickly

- If it's not so urgent, you might want to give it to someone who is not necessarily the obvious choice – on the grounds that it will help him/her to acquire some new skill or gain some new experience.

As a manager, you need to produce short-term results – to get the work done as effectively and efficiently as you can – but you also need to take every opportunity to develop the longer term potential of your team.

One of the perks of being a manager is the ability to delegate work that is really boring! But don't overdo it. A manager who always keeps all the interesting stuff for himself/herself won't be very popular with the team. If a member of your team has been carrying out a succession of routine tasks, find something you can delegate that's more interesting and more challenging.

Letting go

When you delegate, give people as much rein as you can. Make very clear what you want done and set the parameters (e.g. deadline, quality standards, resources). But – and this is a cardinal rule of delegation - leave the person to whom you are delegating to decide how it will be done. Give them any necessary back-up (e.g. documents, speaking to or emailing heads of the departments they'll need to contact) and check that they understand the task. Then stand back and let them get on with it.

It's an art rather than a science - knowing when to step in and when to leave the team to get on with it. It's a judgment that comes only with experience. If the team leader is constantly intervening and interfering it's bound to affect the team's confidence. Allow them to make the occasional mistake. Just leave them to get on with it. Seeing that you believe in them and trust them will work wonders for their confidence.

Fighting for your team

It's important to fight for your team. You should be their champion, both inside and outside the organization. Look after their interests, and pull out all the stops in getting them the best resources. If you don't, they'll see what others get, they'll resent it, and they'll be demotivated. If you want your team to be the best, treat them as the best.

Giving them the credit – and taking the blame

Let the team take all the credit. It really helps to motivate them – and, as their manager, some of it is bound to rub off on you anyway. On the other hand, if the team makes a mess of things, take the blame yourself. After all, it's your team. And nothing generates more loyalty.

Don't forget

Remember that people often learn more from their mistakes than they do from their successes. So have confidence in them.

Rewarding success

If the team has had a big success, it's important to recognize and reward it. How you do that will depend to some extent on the culture of your organization. Any financial rewards will be determined by the organization's use of performance pay, special bonuses and so on.

Regardless of that, the team leader needs to make a point of congratulating people - and making sure that any major success is recognized and acknowledged more widely within the organization. If success means a feather in the cap for the team leader, (s)he should not begrudge treating the team to a celebratory drink or meal. And if the team have put in a superhuman effort without getting the result you wanted, you can still reward them for the effort.

Very few people are motivated mainly by money. That may come as a surprise, but it's true. For most people, job satisfaction, security of employment, status and recognition, feeling appreciated, and prospects for future advancement are all more important than the salary. So don't feel that if you can't give your team more money, you can't motivate them. There are many, many other ways.

Making sure they know what's expected of them

People need to know what's expected of them. Setting clear tasks and objectives is an important part of that. But the manager also has a responsibility to make sure that his/her people understand the organization's culture and the standards of conduct and behavior that are expected.

Of course, the very best way to do this is to model the kind of behavior you are seeking to inculcate into others.

Helping the team to grow

Try to begin by working on problems that immediately resonate with team members. This will help to build trust and understanding. Gradually the team will learn how to make optimum use of their diverse experience and expertise and different perspectives. This will help the team to grow.

Letting the team decide

Sometimes you'll need to get your team to do something that they don't really like. That's life: we can't spend all our time just doing the things we enjoy. But try not to force them to use a method, a system or an approach to which they are fundamentally opposed. If they don't really believe in it, their heart won't be in it and the chances are they won't put in 100% effort. Make sure they know the result you're expecting them to produce but, if you possibly can, leave them to decide how they'll get there.

Every manager a leader

Many management gurus make a clear distinction between leadership and management. I'm not altogether comfortable with that. Obviously, if you're at the top of an organization, it's vital to have a clear vision of the future, and to know where the organization is going and how it's going to get there. But a key component of leadership – to my mind, the most important of all - is the ability to motivate people. And that is something that every manager, however junior, needs - even if (s)he is responsible for managing just one member of staff.

Talking to your team

Go out of your way to discuss important issues and news with your team. Ask what they think and get their opinions. Even if you know more about the subject than they do, asking for their views will make them feel good. It will increase their self-esteem and this might even have a spin-off benefit in terms of improved performance. They will learn from conversations about current issues and key developments. You might learn something too.

Praising the team

Praise is a powerful way of motivating people. Being told that you have done a job really well can increase job satisfaction and make you feel good about yourself. But praise does not have to be given retrospectively. You can tell someone that you're sure they are going to do a really good job before they have done it. If you do that, you'll be saying (implicitly, if not explicitly) that you have confidence in them and that they have what it takes (the necessary skills, experience…whatever) to produce an excellent result. Do that and, believe it or not, you'll almost certainly increase the chances that they will do really well and get the result you need. They won't want to let you – or themselves – down.

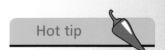

Hot tip

Give the team all the credit.

Team Aims, Objectives and Characteristics

Defining the team's role

The team's role needs to be crystal clear. Everyone needs to understand exactly:

1 what its remit is

2 where it sits in the organizational structure, and

3 to whom it is responsible

You'll need to consider how its work will affect, or be affected by, what others elsewhere in the organization are doing; to avoid any duplication or overlap; and to ensure that others take account of the team's activities. If there is any likelihood of demarcation disputes, it's best to get these sorted out at the outset.

Defining the team's objectives

It's vital that every member of the team has a clear understanding both of the team's objectives and of what (s)he personally is expected to contribute.

Begin by establishing team outputs which are **SMART** (specific, measurable, agreed and achievable, relevant and time-limited). The clearer and more specific these are, the better, and the easier it will be to monitor and evaluate the team's performance.

Team characteristics

- a clear identity

- clear objectives

- clarity about roles and responsibilities

- accountability as a team

- keeping one another fully informed

- honesty and openness

- shared rewards

- mutual respect

- helping one another to develop

- acceptance of common rules and discipline

- mutual support

- sharing professional knowledge

- learning from other team members

- making the best use of complementary skills and experience

- pooling ideas and using the best

- sharing problems

- bouncing ideas off people who speak the same language

Team Roles

Identifying the skills and experience you need

If you're setting up a team from scratch, consider what experience and skills you'll need:

1 go through each of the team's objectives in turn

2 think about the main tasks that will have to be undertaken, and

3 identify the specific competencies needed.

If that sounds easy enough, don't be fooled. You'll probably find that you have some of the necessary experience and skills in abundance - alongside some gaping holes. If resources are limited (and they will be) you'll have to make some compromises. For example, you might decide to exclude someone who has first-rate technical skills, on the grounds that someone else has adequate technical skills alongside other attributes (such as strong interpersonal skills) which will be of greater overall benefit to the team. If you can't get all the skills you need within the team itself, you may have to settle for obtaining some of them from outside as and when you need them.

Seeing who can play which team role(s)

The work of Dr Meredith Belbin (author of Team Roles at Work (1993)) has identified nine team roles, each with its strengths and weaknesses. Importantly, Belbin recognizes that most people have more than one preferred team role: typically they have three or four roles which they can adopt as the situation requires. Some of the key characteristics covered by the nine roles described in Belbin's model are:

- Creative and imaginative

- Enthusiastic and communicative

- Goals-oriented and decision-focused

- Dynamic and determined

- Strategic and capable of accurate judgment

- Cooperative and team-oriented

- Disciplined and practical

- Painstaking and conscientious

- Having specialist knowledge and skills

Using analytical psychology to define personality traits

Carl Jung, a Swiss psychiatrist who developed a unique system of analytical psychology, observed that people relate to the world in four different ways:

- intellectually

- emotionally

- imaginatively

- physically

Jung's observation can be translated into broad personality traits along the following lines:

- (the capability to) approach problems logically and objectively

- take account of the human dimension and the way people feel

- come up with imaginative solutions

- promote those solutions to the outside world

A team needs all these four capabilities.

Differences in working styles

Jung's work has led to the development of personality profiling models (one of the best known is Myers Briggs) to help people understand differences in working styles. It's important to recognize that these models are non-judgmental: they describe working preferences – not skills or abilities. They reflect normal differences between healthy people!

...cont'd

Here are some examples:

- If you have an extrovert style, you'll prefer to develop ideas through discussion, talk through problems, speak or act first and reflect later, and communicate orally. With an introvert style, you'll prefer to develop ideas internally and think through problems, focus on the task and work without interruption, reflect before speaking, and communicate in writing.

- In dealing with information, you'll either (a) collect specific facts and evidence before reaching a conclusion, and have a practical, realistic approach to problems, or (b) prefer to focus on the big picture, and be interested in ideas and new challenges.

- In making decisions, you'll either (a) weigh up the evidence logically, apply consistent principles and reach an objective conclusion, or (b) decide issues on the basis of your own values and beliefs, and try to accommodate others and reach consensus.

- In managing yourself and your work, you'll either (a) be methodical and organized, enjoy decision-making and like to get things settled quickly, or (b) feel restricted by schedules and timescales, like to be spontaneous, and prefer to keep your options open.

Human beings are complicated creatures. Most people have a mixture of personality traits and working styles, and do not fit neatly into little boxes. So be a little skeptical about all this stuff. However, Belbin's team role theory, Jung's work and models based on it can help you to:

- understand yourself and your own behavior better

- appreciate the impact of your behavior on others

- adapt your working style to accommodate others, and

- see that it can be useful to approach issues in different ways

Appraising Individual Performance

Key principles

Most organizations have a system for appraising individual performance at least once a year. The detailed procedures vary, but we can identify some key principles:

Don't forget

Provide continuous feedback on performance – not just once a year.

- **Provide continuous feedback:** the annual appraisal should not come as a nasty shock! If someone has made a bad mistake or produced poor work, it is best if the manager points this out immediately – not for the purpose of apportioning blame, but in order to get the individual to recognize that something has gone wrong and to help him/her to ensure that it does not happen again. Similarly, if someone has produced an excellent piece of work, congratulate him/her immediately. When you give feedback, avoid generalities: it's very important to be specific and factual. Whether the feedback is positive or negative, substantiate it by giving concrete examples.

- **Seek input from the job holder:** the person doing the job knows more about it than anyone else! Involving the job holder in the process gives him/her some control over his/her work - a key factor in obtaining commitment.

- **Attack the problem, not the person:** objective identification of problems and rational discussion (both of the facts and of possible solutions) should help both the manager and the job holder to address issues constructively and to arrive at an agreed solution.

- **Prepare thoroughly for the appraisal meeting:** both manager and job holder need to assemble facts and evidence to support their view of performance achieved during the past year, and to think about tasks and objectives for the year ahead.

...cont'd

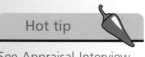

Hot tip

See Appraisal Interview checklist on page 177.

The discussion itself should have four phases:

1. Review what has been achieved during the past year and compare this with the tasks and objectives agreed at the beginning of the year.

2. Identify and explore factors, both internal and external, which have affected performance (for good or bad). Don't let this become antagonistic or recriminatory: the manager's key skills here are questioning and active listening.

3. Agree new tasks and objectives: it is usually best if these are proposed by the job holder. They can then be discussed and changed as necessary in order to agree a list which meets the needs both of the manager and of the job holder.

4. Identify training and development needs: it is often useful to divide these into short-term (training) requirements, to help the individual improve performance in the current job, and longer term needs related to future career development.

...cont'd

Tasks and objectives should be:

- linked to organizational objectives

- listed in priority order

- specific

- measurable (quantity and time are often the most useful measures)

- challenging but realistic

360 degree appraisal

This form of appraisal involves receiving feedback on performance not only from the individual's manager, but also from subordinates, colleagues at the same level, and others for whom work is done or to whom a service is provided.

360 degree feedback is being introduced in an increasing number of organizations, particularly at senior levels. It tends to give the job holder a pretty accurate idea of how (s)he is perceived, but it needs to be handled extremely carefully and sensitively.

It is usual for the feedback to be filtered for confidentiality, so that the job holder cannot identify the comments of specific individuals, and to be channeled through a third party.

Beware

360 degree appraisal can be useful, but it needs to be handled sensitively.

Don't forget

Questioning and listening are the most important skills a manager needs in conducting a review of individual performance.

Training

Knowledge, competencies, professional development, teaching of vocational or prac practical skills provides the b
- On-the-job training take
- Off-the-job training aw

Training and development

Training and development can help any team to fulfill its potential. Training is about acquiring or improving the skills people need to do their current work. Development is about helping them to move on – to learn the skills and gain the experience they'll need in the next job and beyond.

Identifying training and development needs should be an integral part of the annual performance appraisal.

Training courses can help - especially if they are high-quality and focused on specific, identified work-related needs.

But consider other options:

- sitting someone alongside a more experienced colleague, whether it's for a couple of days or just a couple of hours

- away-days where the team can learn from one another, perhaps by tackling a problematic issue

- outside visits that enable people to see how their work fits into the wider context

- job swaps; attachments or secondments to other organizations

- special one-off projects that can provide new experience or an opportunity to learn new skills

...cont'd

Coaching is another option. A coach is usually a training and development expert who helps individuals on a one-to-one basis, typically by taking him/her through questions along the following lines:

Hot tip

See *Business Coaching in easy steps*

- what's the problem – what do you want to achieve here?

- what's the background – what are the facts?

- what are your options?

- what action can you take, and how can obstacles be overcome?

A good coach helps the individual to find out what works for him/her.

Good Practice

The real team player

Are you a real team player? Not just someone who goes through the motions? It's not unknown for people to pay lip-service to team-working while taking every opportunity to promote their own personal interests at the expense of the team.

If the team is to be an effective force, all team members need to pull in the same direction. If one person bad-mouths the team, its leader or other team members to people outside the team, that's bound to reflect badly on the whole team. If it continues for any length of time, morale will suffer. If you're in a team, it's your duty to support, promote and even fight for the team.

Don't wash dirty linen in public – but wash it

No team is perfect. You may well have gripes about the way the team or its leader operates, or about the way a particular issue or a particular project is being handled. Don't be tempted to give vent to your feelings in front of an outside audience.

Being a member of a team is a bit like being in Government! You can have all the arguments and disagreements you like within the team. But once you're facing the outside world, it's your duty to present a common front.

On the other hand, if you're unhappy about the way things are being done or if something is going seriously wrong, don't hesitate to speak up about it within the team. Try to do this in a constructive way: if something isn't working, suggest an alternative that you believe would work.

The team as family

Families are not always harmonious, but one of the characteristics of stable, enduring family relationships is a willingness to support and protect other family members against the outside world.

Mutual support, help and protection is an important characteristic of successful teams. If someone else in the team is under pressure, try to help out. You might need some help yourself one day.

Beware

Don't criticize the team or individual team members in public.

Sharing information

Information is power. But that does not mean that you should keep it all to yourself. If you don't share what you know with those around you, they're unlikely to share what they know with you.

In fact, no team can operate effectively and efficiently unless its members are prepared to share what they know. For example, everyone should know, at least in general terms, what projects or tasks others are working on.

If one person picks up an important piece of news, it should be shared with the rest of the team. Then, if that person is suddenly taken ill, the information won't be lost to the rest of the world.

A brief email can be a good way of passing on information, especially if members of the team spend a lot of time away from the office.

Conflict

If there's conflict within the team, don't ignore it. It needs to be addressed and worked through. Conflict can arise for any number of reasons.

- differences of opinion about the way the team operates

- the way a specific problem or project is being handled

- clashes of personality

Whatever the reason, the team leader needs to grasp the nettle and talk it through with the rest of the team. That may be uncomfortable, but once it has been done the team will be stronger and healthier and will have a much better chance of achieving its objectives.

Beware

Don't ignore personality clashes or conflict within the team.

Summary

- A team is a group of people with complementary skills, experience and roles, who work together to achieve common and agreed aims

- The team leader must lead by example – walk the talk

- Get to know what makes each member of your team tick

- Take every opportunity to praise the team and make them feel good about themselves

- Make sure the team know the result you're expecting, but leave them to decide how they'll get there

- Every manager who has any staff management responsibilities is a leader

- Every member of the team must be clear about the team's aims and objectives and about what he/she is expected to contribute

- Team objectives should be SMART (specific, measurable, achievable and agreed, relevant and time-limited)

- Belbin's work can help to ensure that all the team roles you need are covered

- Profiling models based on Jung's analysis can help to identify personality traits and to ensure that your team has a mix of different working styles

- Apply the key principles of individual performance assessment set out at pages 107–109

- Take every opportunity to train and develop the team

8 Managing Negotiations

Most managers are involved in negotiations of one kind or another. To negotiate effectively you need to have a clear objective and to be prepared to give as well as to take.

Beware

Negotiating service contracts or to resolve policy differences is not the same as buying a second-hand car.

Don't forget

Think long term.

Objectives

Types of negotiations

These days any manager is likely to be involved, sooner or later, in negotiations of one kind or another - perhaps over such things as budgets, pay, staffing, office accommodation and so on. There may be disagreements about policies or priorities, or demarcation disputes between different departments.

These discussions are not always called "negotiations", but very often you'll find that in order to arrive at a solution which everyone can accept, you need to settle for less than you would ideally like. You need to give and take - in other words, to negotiate.

Most organizations contract out a whole range of support services – things like office cleaning, travel, transport, IT support, training, security, catering and so on. Someone has to negotiate all those contracts. If you're in sales you probably have to negotiate with customers or agents about prices, delivery dates, commission rates, etc. If your organization has overseas operations or interests you may find yourself involved in international negotiations.

These scenarios are all very different, but the principles and techniques of effective negotiation apply to all of them.

Thinking long term

If you're buying a second-hand car, or arguing with a salesman at the door, or haggling over a piece of junk at a car boot sale, negotiating is pretty straightforward. You just decide how much you are prepared to pay. Then you offer less than that. Your sole aim is to get the best deal you can. If you're able to persuade the seller to accept less than you know the object is worth, you'll probably feel very pleased with yourself.

If the seller subsequently realizes that you've made a fool of him, it really doesn't matter. The chances are, you'll never see him again.

When a manager is negotiating, things are rather different. It doesn't matter much whether the negotiation is internal or with an external contractor or other organization. Whoever you're negotiating with, shafting the opposition is unlikely to be a good idea. You'll almost certainly have to deal with them in the future.

If you pull a fast one on them today, they may do the same to you tomorrow. You need to get the best deal you can, of course, but it's usually a good idea to ensure that the other party also gets something out of the negotiation. If you can do that, you have a much better chance of building a long-term, mutually beneficial relationship.

What do you want to achieve?

The first principle of negotiation is to be absolutely clear about your objective – what is it that you want to get out of it? Sounds obvious, doesn't it? But if it's a tricky or a very complex subject and you're pressed for time, it's all too easy to arrive at a meeting with only a very fuzzy idea of what it is that you are seeking. And that's a recipe for disaster.

Of course, it's possible that you'll have to modify your objective – for example, if some new information comes to light, or if you're faced with facts or arguments which make it unsustainable. But it's imperative to begin with a very clear idea about what you want to achieve.

Preparation and Negotiating Positions

Ideal outcome, fall-back, bottom line

Hot tip

See Negotiation check list on page 178.

- If, for one reason or another, you're in a very strong negotiating position, you might get close to achieving your ideal outcome. But that's pretty unlikely. In practice, however strong your arguments, the chances are you won't get everything you want.

- So you need to have a realistic fall-back position – something you could live with which you believe has a realistic chance of being acceptable to the others parties to the negotiation. You may need to do some detective work so that you can make an educated guess about others' negotiating positions.

- Finally, it's important to work out your bottom line – the absolute minimum that you can accept. This is the line in the sand beyond which you will not go, whatever concessions are offered or whatever pleas or threats are made. This is the point at which you refuse to be party to any agreement.

Being realistic

Clarity about your objective and your negotiating position – the ideal outcome, the fall-back and the bottom line – is the first (but only the first) step in preparing for any negotiation. Here I'd like to inject a dose of hard reality, based on personal experience. For six years I was the UK's representative to one of the Council Working Groups that meet in Brussels to hammer out differences between members of the European Union. I was involved in lots of negotiations, and there were often huge differences between the participants. On only one occasion did I get close to achieving the ideal outcome. Usually, the result was somewhere between the fall-back position and the bottom line – and it was often closer to the bottom line.

An agreed position

If the subject of the negotiation is of minor importance, or if the result will affect only you and your team, you can probably work out your negotiating position without reference to anyone else. But if your role is to represent your department, you need to make sure that your negotiating stance has been agreed by key stakeholders in the department. The same applies, to an even greater extent, if you are representing your whole organization. You'll almost certainly need to have some internal discussions and negotiations in order to get all the key people on board and signed up to an agreed line.

These internal negotiations are sometimes the most difficult of all. When I worked at the Department of Trade and Industry and represented UK interests at EU negotiations in Brussels, the preparatory discussions between different Whitehall departments, thrashing out an agreed UK negotiating position, were sometimes more difficult than the subsequent negotiations in Brussels.

Negotiating mandate

There are few things more frustrating to a negotiator than to discover that the person(s) (s)he is negotiating with does not have the authority to agree to anything! It's bad enough if this is discovered at the outset of a meeting, but even worse if it emerges only at the end of the negotiation, after you thought you had a done deal. Sometimes it might be appropriate and useful to have preparatory discussions, perhaps at a lower level, at which the parties to the negotiation can exchange preliminary views and see how much common ground there is, before the negotiations proper begin. But if that is the case, everyone needs to be crystal clear about the basis of the discussions. If you're a negotiator, you need to have a mandate to negotiate.

Thorough preparation

1. Make sure, before you go into the negotiation, that you have a real understanding of the subject matter.

2. Take time to brief yourself thoroughly. You'll need to look at previous papers or reports; you may need to talk to colleagues who've been involved in the past; or to consult experts or specialists, inside or outside your organization, who know more about the subject than you do.

3. Make sure that you have all the relevant facts and figures at your fingertips, and that you really know your stuff. The better prepared you are, the greater your chances of success.

Don't forget

Discussions to resolve disagreements may not always be called "negotiations", but the same principles and techniques apply.

Informal Contacts

Finding out what the others think

To negotiate effectively you need to know something about the negotiating position of the people on the other side of the table. That's not always easy, but more often than not a glance at the relevant papers or a few phone calls will throw some light on the approach they are likely to adopt.

If you can get some clues about their attitude, you should be able to make some sort of guess about the points they're likely to make and to think about how you can deal with them.

Getting beneath the surface

Those you are negotiating with will probably take up a position and use all the facts and arguments they can muster to defend that position.

If it's an important negotiation the line they take will have been agreed at a high level within their organization, and they may have little or no room for maneuver. They're unlikely to say much, if anything, about what lies behind their negotiating position.

In order to have any realistic chance of persuading them to change that position, you need to probe beneath the surface. You need to understand the pressures they are under and the interests and concerns they are seeking to protect.

Almost certainly, you won't be able to do that during the negotiation itself – especially if there are lots of participants, all representing different interests and all with different axes to grind. No-one is likely to be too forthcoming in front of a big audience.

Tête-à-tête

On the other hand, if you can have a quiet chat, one-to-one, with the main parties to the negotiation, they may well be prepared to be a little more open about the pressures they are under and the underlying concerns and interests they are seeking to protect.

Obviously, if you're going on a fishing expedition for this kind of information, you'll have to be prepared to say something about the interests and concerns behind your own negotiating position. But that's what's involved in any negotiation – you have to give as well as to take.

Hot tip

Put as much effort into informal, one-to-one discussions as into the formal meeting.

Getting to know them

It's easier to negotiate if you know the people you're negotiating with. So it's worthwhile taking the trouble to get to know them.

It's often a good idea to arrive a few minutes early so that you can have an informal word or two with people before the serious business begins. Even if you're just exchanging pleasantries or chatting about the latest political scandal, it can help to break the ice.

If you can establish some kind of personal rapport with the people around the table, you'll probably feel more relaxed and this will make it easier for you to get your points across. It will also help to promote the kind of friendly, constructive atmosphere in which any negotiation is most likely to succeed.

Informal discussions

The more negotiations I was involved with in Brussels, the more I realized the value of informal contacts and quiet, one-to-one discussions. Sometimes these took place in the corner of the meeting room, but more often it was over a coffee or a beer or over lunch in the canteen.

When negotiations became really difficult and there were huge differences of approach, it was very rare that these differences were settled in the conference room.

More often, informal, often bilateral, discussions eventually resulted in some softening of positions and enabled the deadlock to be broken.

If you are dealing with complex issues, this can be a slow, painstaking process. But whether the negotiation is simple and straightforward or complex and difficult, informal contacts and one-to-one discussions are often the key to success.

Hot tip

Make a real effort to get to know the people you're negotiating with.

Don't forget

Any situation in which you have to give as well as take is a negotiation.

Tactics

Using meeting and presentation skills

Some of the tips given in Chapter 3 (Managing Presentations) and Chapter 4 (Managing Meetings) apply also to negotiations. You need to get your points across clearly and succinctly. You need to make an impact. You need to listen very carefully to what others are saying: you may need to read between the lines. If you don't understand something, ask questions and seek clarification. When you speak yourself, try to use specific examples to back up your arguments.

Knowing when to listen and when to speak

You need to think about when and how you intervene in the discussion. You might want to get in early so that you can set the agenda, influence the direction of the discussion, and focus on those aspects that are of particular importance to you. Or you might want to keep your powder dry: to hear what others have to say first, so that you are in a better position to counter their arguments. Based on what you know about the subject, about how the negotiation is going to be handled, and – not least – about the other people around the table, you have to decide which tactics will enable you to make your case most effectively. It's your call.

Linkages

At high-level negotiations, when the stakes are high, linkages may be made, especially during the end-game, between totally unrelated issues: "OK, we've reached agreement on X. But I'm only going to sign up to it if you give me what I want on Y". A linkage of that kind can be difficult to deal with. The best hope of avoiding or dealing effectively with it is to have:

- an in-depth understanding of the interests and motivations of your negotiating partner

- close personal contacts and a good rapport with your negotiating partner(s)

- a clear understanding of the importance your organization attaches to the issue on which you're negotiating and of how it fits into the bigger picture of its overall interests

- an unrelated demand of your own up your sleeve, so that if necessary you can use this as a countervailing bargaining counter

In Writing

At the end of the negotiation it's vital for everyone to have a clear, agreed understanding of what has (and, perhaps, what has not) been agreed. Someone needs to sum up the result, going through everything that has been agreed in as much detail as is necessary to avoid any possibility of misunderstanding.

Negotiations at the very highest levels sometimes break up with different participants having a rather different understanding of what has been agreed.

Make sure this does not happen to you.

1   Take care to ensure that the detail of exactly what has been agreed is recorded in writing and circulated to all the participants

2   It's best for this to be done immediately the negotiation is concluded, even if the detail has to be incorporated into a formal contract, agreement or other document that will be drawn up at a later date

Summary

- There are many types of negotiation, but the same principles and techniques can be applied to all of them

- Be clear about your negotiating objective

- Get the best result you can, but look to build a long-term relationship

- Be prepared to give as well as take

- Have a fall-back position and a bottom line

- Prepare thoroughly and make sure you have all the relevant facts and arguments at your finger tips

- Get to know the people you're negotiating with

- Probe beneath the surface to find out what interests your negotiating partners are seeking to promote or protect

- Informal, one-to-one discussions are often the key to success

- Use your meeting and presentation skills to argue your case as clearly, succinctly and convincingly as you can

- Don't give in to attempted linkages with unrelated issues

- Make sure you know what's been agreed and get it down in writing

9 Managing Decisions

If you're a manager, decision-taking comes with the territory. Some are small and some are big. The more senior you are, the more decisions you're likely to have to take, and the more difficult they'll be.

Hot tip

Use objective criteria to evaluate options, and bear in mind that some criteria will be more important than others.

Introduction

If you're a manager, you can't avoid taking decisions. Some, such as approving someone's holiday plans or expense claims, are minor; and some are major – for example, deciding whether to go ahead with an important project, or recruiting a key member of your team. Some are easy and some are difficult. Some can be taken quickly and some require a great deal of thought and, perhaps, consultation with others. Decisions come in all shapes and sizes.

As you become more senior, you'll have to take an increasing number of critical decisions.

● As you progress higher up the organization, it becomes ever more important to see the big picture - to take account of the wider political, economic, social and environmental context.

● If you get to the very top, you'll be taking decisions that have a major impact on your organization and those who work for it – and, quite probably, on the outside world.

If you have to take a tricky decision, put your subjective thoughts to one side and consider the matter objectively and professionally, on the basis of the facts.

Whose decision?

Before you take the decision, make sure you are the right person to take it.

● Is the subject matter one in which another part of your organization has a greater interest? If so, it may be more sensible to get someone in another department to take the decision, feeding in any relevant facts or arguments you may have.

● If the decision clearly falls within your bailiwick, consider whether it's one you can delegate to a member of your team.

● Perhaps it's a decision your boss will expect to take, or at least to be consulted about? If that's the case, try to get into the habit of giving him/her your own views and saying what decision you recommend.

Consultation

Once you're clear that you are the right person to take the decision, think about whether or not you need to consult others. That will depend upon

- the complexity of the subject matter

- who will be affected by it

You might need to seek the views of other members of your team, or to consult people elsewhere in the organization – or outside.

How to consult

If you do need to consult others, take a moment to consider the best way of doing this.

- In some cases a simple phone call might suffice

- If the issue is more substantive or more complex, you'll probably need to seek views in writing, perhaps by email - in this event, it's always advisable to set a deadline

- If you conclude that the issue needs to be discussed thoroughly, and that different parts of the organization need to be given an opportunity to express their views before you take the decision, you'll probably need to call a meeting

Hot tip

Brainstorming can be used to produce a wide range of options.

Hot tip

See Option Appraisal checklist on page 179.

Don't forget

Think through the consequences of your decision.

Options

Thinking creatively

If you're faced with a difficult decision, it's sensible to look at how similar issues or problems have been dealt with in the past. Think about who may have been faced with this problem before. Sometimes the precedent will provide the answer, but it's not a good idea to be constrained by what happened in the past. The circumstances may have changed. Look at the issue with a fresh pair of eyes. Think laterally.

Identifying options

If the decision is a simple one, there may be only two options: to say either yes or no. If it's more complex, there may be several possible reactions. If that's the case, you need to weigh up the options before you take a decision.

1. The first thing to do is to identify all the possible ways of dealing with the problem. One way of doing this is to "brainstorm" the issue – to get together with your team and/or your colleagues who are most involved, and come up with as many options as possible. Don't try to evaluate these during the brainstorming session itself. Just let ideas flow as fast and as freely as you can, however impracticable or off-the-wall they might be.

2. Once the initial brainstorming session has ended, stand back and allow people to discuss the ideas they've come up with. At this point you'll probably agree to dismiss some of them out of hand. But someone's apparently crazy idea might light a spark in someone else, stimulating discussion and perhaps leading to the identification of something that could really work. With any luck you'll end up with a short list of viable options.

Pros and cons

Once you have identified viable options, you need to consider each one in turn, identifying its pros and cons. For each option, there are bound to be both advantages and disadvantages. Just put them all down methodically, either on paper or on a flip chart.

Evaluation criteria

Once you have identified the options and listed the pros and cons of each one, you need to weigh them, one against the other. To do this, you need to establish criteria – to decide which factors you will take into account in comparing one option with another. The criteria you select will depend on the subject matter. They might, for example, include such things as

- cost

- practicability

- acceptability to staff

- stakeholder reactions

- speed of implementation.

It's often the case that some criteria are more important than others.

1 You can reflect this by giving a different weighting to each of your chosen criteria, perhaps using a scale of 1-5.

2 Then you can evaluate each of your options according to the extent to which it satisfies or does not satisfy each of the criteria, perhaps awarding points on a scale of 0-10.

3 If you multiply the latter by the weighting given to each criterion, you'll be able to see which of your options best meets your criteria.

But don't be over-reliant on the arithmetic. If there is not much to choose between, say, your top two or three options, don't be afraid to be guided, in the final analysis, by experience and common sense – and sheer gut instinct.

Hot tip

Consider the issue objectively, on the basis of the facts.

Consequences

Stakeholders

Before you take a final decision, think through what effect it will have on your key stakeholders. You might want to glance back at Chapter 5 (Managing Projects) and use the stakeholder analysis techniques described there. Once you are clear about who the stakeholders are and how they will be affected by your decision, you can consider how to handle them. You might want to seek their views or even to involve them in the decision-making process.

Risks

Some decisions are routine and virtually risk-free. But if it's an important decision, it's worthwhile considering what, if any, risks are involved.

Beware

The effects of putting off a decision can be worse than those of taking it.

- If the decision does involve significant risks, you can analyze these for probability and impact, as described in Chapter 5

- If you conclude that the risks of your preferred decision are just too great, you might have to consider alternative options

- If you decide that all the possible options involve unacceptable risks, you'll have to think about the risks involved in taking no decision

Once you have reached a decision, think through the consequences before you put it into effect. Try to get into the habit of doing this as a matter of course, however big or small the decision. If you're tempted to put it off, consider what effect that will have.

Once the decision has been taken, put it into effect without delay. Don't prevaricate. In the long run, the downside of putting off difficult decisions is often worse than the consequences of taking decisive action. Even if people don't agree with your decision, they'll probably respect you for taking it.

Implementation

Communicating your decision

Don't forget to communicate your decision to those affected by it. Lack of effective communication is one of the commonest causes of misunderstandings and confusion in any organization.

If people aren't told about a decision that affects them, you'll store up trouble for the future. Think carefully about how and when to communicate it. If it's a sensitive issue, you'll need to handle it with great care.

Putting the decision into effect

It's often easier to take a decision than to ensure that it is implemented effectively. Make sure that the necessary follow-up action is taken.

Implementation of a big decision, such as going ahead with a new project or adopting a new policy, may involve use of some of the project management tools and techniques described in Chapter 5. Mechanisms will have to be put in place for monitoring progress and for ensuring that the project or policy is put into effect within budget, on time and to the required standard.

Don't assume that once you have taken the decision, that's the end of the matter. It might only be the beginning.

Hot tip

Put aside personal prejudices and subjective opinions.

Don't forget

Remember to communicate your decision to those who will be affected.

Don't forget

Implementation is often the most difficult part of any decision.

Summary

- Put your subjective thoughts to one side and consider the issue objectively and professionally, on the basis of the facts

- Effective decision-taking requires experience, common sense and good judgment

- Make sure you're the right person to take the decision

- Consider the need to consult other people

- Think creatively

- Identify the options, and consider the pros and cons of each one

- Establish criteria and evaluate the options

- Identify risks (if any) and consider their probability and potential impact

- Think about how stakeholders will be affected

- Don't put off difficult decisions

- Pay attention to the way your decision is communicated

- Make sure the decision is implemented effectively

10 Managing Change

To survive and prosper, an organization needs to improve continuously and to adapt to the changing world around it. If it doesn't change, it can't improve.

Beware

Most people find change unsettling.

Hot tip

See EFQM Excellence Model on page 180.

Hot tip

See Balanced Scorecard on page 181.

Hot tip

See SWOT Analysis on page 182–183.

Change and Continuity

Why change?

"It is not the strongest of the species that survive, nor the most intelligent, but the most responsive to change." That's what Charles Darwin said.

There are many reasons why an organization may need to make major changes. Among the most common are:

- **Political** factors: a change of government or of government policies; major international developments.

- **Economic** factors: major national macro-economic developments; taxation; changes in interest and/or exchange rates; significant market trends.

- **Social** factors: demographic changes; ethnic and/or religious factors; changes in educational levels; lifestyle trends.

- **Technological** factors: innovation; research; new IT developments; patents and intellectual property.

- **Environmental** factors: climate change; natural phenomena (e.g. earthquakes, hurricanes, floods); ecological and conservation issues; infrastructure (e.g. energy, roads, rail); waste management.

- **Legal** factors: employment law; international law and treaties; anti-corruption measures; any new government legislation affecting the organization.

An organization may need to change in order to adjust to changes (such as the examples given above) in the external environment. It may also need to change as a result of unfavorable comparisons with prevailing best practice.

Self-assessment (perhaps based on an assessment tool such as the EFQM Excellence Model or the balanced scorecard) may have shown that the organization needs to:

- reinforce and build on its strengths

- address weaknesses

- exploit new opportunities

- deal with perceived threats or risks

Change as the norm

Increasingly, change is the norm – whatever work you do and whatever kind of organization you work for. And every year the pace and frequency of change seems to increase.

The world does not stand still, and any organization needs to adapt to the changing environment if it is to survive and prosper. Continuous improvement is the name of the game.

You may be faced with a massive upheaval – a major change in the way your organization is structured, or the way it works. Or you might have to implement some small changes to the way things are done.

Sometimes relatively small adjustments to systems or working practices can result in a significant cumulative improvement in effectiveness and efficiency.

Constant change and reorganization often does more harm than good.

- institutional memory is lost

- everyone worries about their future rather than the job they're doing, and

- no-one really understands what's happening

Most people find change unsettling. It has to be handled sensitively. One of the hallmarks of an effective manager is:

- the ability to adapt

- the ability to help others to adapt to changed circumstances

Beware

Continuous upheaval will demotivate the workforce.

Big bang change

Introducing huge change, involving massive upheaval, in one fell swoop can have advantages (as well as disadvantages). It has an immediate impact.

- It signals a clear break with the past – which may be appropriate if new leadership wants to start with a new broom and clear away old principles or working practices

- It may guarantee speedy implementation of the desired changes, and set a clear direction for the future

- In some circumstances – a sudden crisis or emergency, for example, or perhaps even a change of government – big bang change is appropriate and necessary

Incremental change

Often it is more appropriate to make changes gradually over a period of time.

- This gives you the opportunity to correct mistakes, and to build on what works

- You can pilot the changes on a small scale and see how they turn out in practice. The chances are, you'll need to make a few changes, or at least to fine tune some of the detail. When you have applied the lessons learnt from the pilot, you're more likely to end up with something that will really work. Then you can roll it out across the board

- You'll have a better chance of embedding and sustaining change across the organization. Sustainability is usually more important than speed

Small-scale, incremental change makes it much easier to involve the workforce. Often it's the people at the coalface, dealing with the day-to-day practicalities, who are best able to spot potential difficulties and suggest how they can be overcome. If the workforce are involved in the planning and implementation of change, they're more likely to be committed to making it

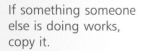

Hot tip

If something someone else is doing works, copy it.

happen. Incremental change also provides greater opportunity for stakeholder consultation and involvement – and that may be the difference between success and failure.

Copying the best

You don't necessarily need to be original. Often all you need to do is to identify the best - and to copy it! This is how many famous painters, musicians and writers learnt their craft. If you come across something that someone else is doing that really works, don't hesitate to copy it.

Key themes

Implementing a program of major organizational change can be a tough challenge for any manager. You'll have an uphill struggle if you don't have a clear understanding of four key themes, and how each of these relates to your own organization and the changes you're seeking to implement. These are:

- leadership

- communication

- strategy

- culture

Hot tip

Effective change requires the wholehearted commitment of top management.

Hot tip

See an excerpt from *Leadership in easy steps* on page 186.

Leadership

Top management

No program of change has much chance of success unless those at the top of the organization are committed to it. I have been involved in change programs, both in the UK and in Central and Eastern Europe, which have failed to produce the results expected simply because, at the end of the day, those at the very top were not committed to them. It's not sufficient for top management to go along passively with a change program: they need to be proactively involved in

- promoting it

- putting it into practice

- modeling the changed actions or behaviors they want others to adopt

The manager's role

Every manager needs to lead the people (s)he manages. If you're implementing major changes:

1. you must explain and sell those changes to your team - and show by your own example that you're committed to putting them into practice

2. you must give your people all the help and support you can

An opportunity, not a threat

The chances are, you won't like every aspect of the changes you have to implement. Perhaps you won't like anything at all about them! Try to look at them – and to get your team to look at them – not as a threat, but as an opportunity. Whatever the nature of the changes, there are bound to be some positive elements. Home in on these.

- Instead of reacting defensively and negatively, think positively.

- Encourage your people to make the most of the opportunity to do things differently. It could give them the chance to demonstrate skills they didn't even know they had.

Communication

Involvement and commitment

Whatever kind of change you're involved with, communicating that change effectively to those who are affected is critically important. It's essential that staff and key stakeholders are informed and consulted. This can be a tricky business, especially if people are not convinced that the change will be in their best interests.

- they need to understand the rationale – to know why the change is taking place and what it is intended to achieve

- they need to know how and when it will be implemented, what effect it will have on them, what the benefits will be

- they need to know what exactly their own role will be in putting it into practice

Bottom-up change

Commitment from those at the top of the organization is a prerequisite for successful change. But if the change is to be more than surface-deep it also needs to be embraced by those at the coal-face lower down the organization.

Staff with practical, day-to-day experience of operational issues often know better than anyone else how to implement change most effectively; and change brought about with the active participation and involvement of the workforce will be far more firmly-rooted than anything imposed from above. So do your utmost to:

- involve people in the practical details of how the changes are put into practice on the ground

- give them some responsibility, and the chances are they'll feel some ownership.

Don't forget

Participation of the workforce in decision-making and implementation can help to ensure that changes are sustainable.

Strategy

Don't forget

Consult key stakeholders about any major change and try to involve them.

In any change situation, clarity of vision and purpose is vital. It's essential for people to have a clear understanding of the organization's strategic direction - to know

- where it is going

- how it's going to get there

Everyone needs to understand clearly

- why change is necessary

- what the benefits will be

- what (s)he is expected to contribute

It's essential to build consensus and gain buy-in. Then, with any luck, everyone will pull in the same direction. The strategic vision will be translated into specific tasks and actions, and these will be implemented effectively throughout the organization.

Culture

Focusing on the little things

Organizational culture is a difficult thing to define. It's really an amalgam of "the way things are done around here".

It is usually taken as including:

- Values

- Beliefs

- Structure

- Control mechanisms

- Rituals

- Routines

- Symbols

- Language

Changing processes and systems is relatively straightforward: it may take time for people to get to grips with new procedures, but with training and on-the-job support it does not usually present insuperable problems.

Organizational culture is more intangible and difficult to pin down. For this reason cultural change is hard to tackle head-on. It's often easier and more productive to focus on the little things – for example, the kind of behaviors and day-to-day routines which the organization is seeking to encourage.

Cultural change is unlikely to be achieved through lecturing or evangelizing. The key influences are more likely to be

- role models

- peer pressure

- clear leadership

as ever, those at the top need to "walk the talk".

Change Management Models

There are many tools, techniques and models that can help you to manage change effectively. Some have been touched on in earlier chapters of this book. There are countless change management models, and they all have their proponents. There is no one-size-fits-all model. Managing major change in the real world is different from, and more difficult than, working through theoretical models, but these can be useful as a reminder of key issues to think about or steps to take. Kotter and McKinsey are two models you might want to take a look at.

Kotter's 8-step change model

John Kotter is a Harvard Business School Professor and author of the book Leading Change (1996). His model of change management has three phases and eight steps, summarized as follows:

Phase One – Defrost the status quo

1. Create a sense of urgency. This is the crucial first step. Around half of all change management programs fail here – because there is no perceived urgency about the need to change.

2. Establish a small group of people who are committed to the change. They must have enough power to lead the change and drive it forward, and they need to work as a team.

3. Develop a compelling view of the desired future.

4. Embody that view in day-to-day activities and lead by example – walk the talk.

Phase Two – Take actions to bring about change

5. Empower employees to implement change – encouraging them to remove obstacles, change processes or systems and adopt new approaches.

6 Generate short-term wins, and reward those responsible.

7 Consolidate improvements and use short-term successes as stepping stones to further change.

Phase Three – Embed the change

8 Fix the change as permanent. Managers at all levels anchor the new approaches in the organization's culture.

McKinsey's 7S framework

This model provides a framework for working through the following key questions (sometimes known as Gap Analysis):

- Where are we now?

- Where do we want to be?

- What's the gap?

The model can be use to aid understanding of the organization and the way it works. It encourages managers seeking to implement change to look at things from the following different angles and perspectives:

1 Strategy

2 Structure

3 Systems

4 Staff

5 Style

6 Shared values

7 Skills

Summary

- If an organization doesn't change, it can't improve

- Increasingly, change is the norm

- Constant change and reorganization can do more harm than good

- For many people, major organizational change is an unsettling experience: it needs to be handled sensitively

- Look at change as an opportunity, not a threat

- Adapting to change – and helping others to adapt – is one of the hallmarks of an effective manager

- A "big bang" approach is sometimes necessary, but incremental change is often more sustainable

- Pay special attention to four critical themes: leadership, communication, strategic direction, and culture

- Successful change requires both leadership from the top and involvement by those at the coalface

- Stakeholder consultation and involvement may be the difference between success and failure

- Models of change management can be useful in identifying critical issues and key steps

- Be clear about where you are now and where you want to get to

11 Managing Delegation

Effective delegation benefits the manager, the delegate and the organization.

Why Delegate?

However brilliant you are, you can't do it all yourself. Delegation allows you to focus on the essential stuff – those tasks that only you can do. By delegating as much day-to-day work as you can, you'll be able to focus on those things that are really important. You should also have more time to devote to strategic issues and to longer-term projects.

Benefits for the manager

In today's environment, when many organizations have to make "efficiency savings" – that often means getting more work out of fewer people – all managers are under pressure to deliver results.

A manager who does not delegate cannot possibly hope to accomplish effectively all the tasks with which he or she is faced. Failure to delegate – or to delegate effectively – means that a manager will spend a lot of time on relatively low-priority work which others could do, and will inevitably have insufficient time and energy to devote to tasks which are really important. The result is likely to be a manager

- who works excessive hours
- is not in control of the work
- seems disorganized

If this kind of situation is allowed to continue, the manager inevitably comes under increasing pressure, and this can result in a heightened level of stress. Delegation eases pressure on the manager.

Short-term pain for long-term gain

Reluctance to delegate may stem from a simple belief that delegation will take longer, and will have a less definite end-result, than doing the work yourself. This may be true. But once you have made the effort and found the time to do it, the process of delegating becomes easier and less time-consuming. And once the delegate has learned how to carry out the new task, the amount of time needed to accomplish it will decrease.

Moreover, in carrying out the task, he or she should learn new skills that will make it easier for the manager to delegate, and the delegate to take on, similar tasks in the future.

Hot tip

Delegation is a manager's best friend – it eases pressure and reduces stress.

Beware

Delegating might take you longer than doing the job yourself – but you'll gain in the long run.

146

The long-term result of effective delegation is

- less pressure on the manager

- more job satisfaction for the delegate

- enhanced performance by the organization

Benefits for the delegate
The stimulus of new responsibilities can be a powerful tool in increasing motivation.

- New tasks successfully accomplished provide a real sense of achievement – a vital element of job satisfaction

- Increased responsibility helps the delegate to broaden his or her experience, learn new skills and build confidence

Benefits for the organization
Effective delegation enables the organization to make optimum use of its human resources. It can:

- improve the morale of staff who have been underemployed

- remove bottlenecks caused by a manager who tries to do too much himself/herself, and

- help to ensure that deadlines are met

- increase the effectiveness and efficiency with which tasks are carried out

- enhance the organization's overall performance

Hot tip

Delegate so that you can spend more time on the important stuff.

Don't forget

Clarity, autonomy and support are the key principles of effective delegation.

Key Principles

Clarity

The first essential is for the manager to be absolutely clear in his or her own mind about

- the task(s) to be delegated

- the results that are required

The tasks need to be clearly identified and the parameters of each one defined.

Once this has been done, the manager needs to ensure that:

- each task

- the results expected

- the deadline by which they are required

are understood by the delegate. It's essential that from the very beginning the manager and the delegate have a clear, agreed understanding of exactly what the task involves and what outcome is expected.

How this clarity is achieved will depend upon the type and complexity of the tasks to be delegated.

- For a relatively simple task a quick and informal oral briefing may well be sufficient. If, despite the simplicity, it's something important, you might want to back this up with a brief note or an email confirming the task you're delegating, the result you expect and the deadline.

- For a more difficult or complex task, you will need to give the delegate a detailed briefing, probably in a one-to-one meeting – and you may want to reinforce this oral briefing with a note underlining the main points. The brief, whether oral or written, should cover any necessary background, the essential information the delegate needs to have in order to carry out the task, the support available, the end-result expected and the deadline. It's very important that there are no uncertainties or ambiguities.

During the briefing meeting pay close attention to the delegate's body language. For example, absence of eye contact may indicate disagreement or reluctance to take on the task, or a lack of understanding about what is required. It's essential that the delegate is given the opportunity to express any concerns he or she may have, so that these can be addressed and dealt with at the outset.

If that is not done, enthusiasm for carrying out the task will diminish, and the chances of achieving the desired outcome will be reduced.

It's important to end the briefing on a positive, upbeat note. Stress that you are delegating the task because you recognize the individual's abilities and have confidence in him or her to carry it out successfully.

Autonomy

Both the manager and the delegate need to have a clear, agreed understanding about how much autonomy the delegate is to have. Usually the best answer to this is: as much as possible.

The ideal way to delegate is:

1 to make absolutely clear what result is expected

2 when it is expected by

3 to leave the delegate to decide exactly how he or she will achieve that result.

Being too prescriptive about the process to be used will limit the possibilities and reduce the scope for initiative. It may inhibit the individual and discourage him or her from going that extra mile and making the contribution they have the potential to make. So, if you possibly can, give the delegate complete autonomy over how the result you want will be achieved. Do that, and the chances are that from time to time you'll be pleasantly surprised to see how much originality and ingenuity your people have.

Hot tip

Give the delegate as much autonomy as you can.

149

...cont'd

So trust them to get on with it. Don't be constantly looking over their shoulders, checking up on them. Let go and leave them to work in their own way. Occasionally they will make mistakes. But that's how they'll learn. A manager who feels the need to keep a close eye on everyone every minute of the day will never get the best out of people. And you'll never get the personal benefits of

● less pressure

● more time

to concentrate on high priority tasks – which a manager should get from effective delegation.

If the delegate is very inexperienced, or if you're asking him or her to undertake a really difficult or complex task for the first time, you might feel the need to give one or two pointers as to how they might proceed.

In these circumstances you'll need to make the delegate feel comfortable with what he or she is being asked to do. If that's the case, try to resist spelling things out in great detail. If you do that, you'll almost certainly be telling them how you yourself would do the job. That's not always such a good idea: believe it or not, there might be better ways of doing it.

● Don't imagine that you always know best, or that you've always got the right answers

● If your delegate comes up with a better way of doing something, don't feel threatened or go into defensive mode

● Welcome anything that will improve your effectiveness and efficiency

● Be prepared to learn and to adapt your own way of working

Both you and the organization will benefit.

Support
In the early stages especially, you'll need to give positive encouragement and support. The most important thing here is to

- emphasize your own interest in and commitment to the piece of work involved

- indicate what support will be available if it's needed

You'll want to stand back and leave your delegate to get on with it. But you'll also want to stress that in the event of any unforeseen opposition, problems or crises, you'll be ready to lend an ear, give your advice and – if absolutely necessary – step in.

- You may need to spell out what human and financial resources (and equipment) will be available to the delegate

- If there are other people, either inside or outside your own organization, who have important and relevant expertise or experience, you will need to ensure that the delegate knows about them

Occasionally, despite carefully considered delegation to the right person with the relevant skills and experience, things will go wrong. That's life. Some unforeseen development will get in the way and prevent the task being completed. When that happens, it's your job to provide effective support.

- Avoid pointing the finger and apportioning blame

- Analyze the circumstances

- Find out exactly what has happened and why

Then discuss the way forward with the delegate and try to agree an action plan that will (a) get over the current difficulty and get the work back on track, and (b) prevent the problem from recurring in the future, either with this piece of work or with some other assignment.

Hot tip

Each social network has its own etiquette and language. If you aren't a regular user, take the time to become familiar with how the groups communicate and what is well received.

Choosing the Delegate

Key factors

Once you have decided to delegate something, whether it's a major project or a routine task, choosing the right person is an important decision. You should give it careful consideration. A number of factors have to be taken into account:

- urgency
- importance
- complexity
- likely duration
- availability of potential candidates
- experience needed
- skills needed
- preferred working style required
- personal development needs

If you're new to the job and you don't really know what your people are capable of, you may have to proceed by trial and error. However, with experience you will quickly learn to assess what's needed for each task that arises, and be able to match it to the right person.

Choice and compromise

Sometimes the urgency of the task and the lack of suitable candidates will limit your options. In those circumstances you'll have to compromise and to choose the person who is available and whose overall experience is in your judgment the most relevant. Remember that your prime responsibility as manager is to get the work done as effectively and quickly as you can.

If the task is not urgent it is often worthwhile considering whether it can be used to broaden someone's experience or to help him or her develop new skills. Learning by doing is often the best way of acquiring or developing any skill. Putting something that's new into practice in a real working environment, where

Beware

Don't always delegate the best stuff to the same person – give everyone a fair crack of the whip.

Don't forget

If it's urgent and important, either do it yourself or delegate it to the best available person.

tasks have to be completed and deadlines have to be met, is far more meaningful, and can provide a deeper and longer-lasting understanding, than any training course.

The way you delegate also needs to be perceived to be fair and rational. There should be no place for subjective judgments or personal prejudice.

● Each task should be analyzed to identify the skills and other attributes that are needed

● Then it should be matched to the best available candidate

But this is often not a precise science. For example, you may decide that one candidate has better technical skills, but that for this particular task, although those technical skills are very desirable, it is more important to have someone who has really good interpersonal skills and is a cooperative team player.

To take another example, someone who works energetically and enthusiastically for a short period of time but loses interest quite quickly, may not be suitable for a long-term project where perseverance and attention to detail will be all-important.

A manager has to delegate in such a way as to get the work done as effectively and efficiently as possible. But both the individual to whom a task is delegated and – equally importantly – those who are not chosen for the task need to understand and accept the rationale. If the most interesting work is always given to the same person, that will inevitably affect the morale and, in the long term, the performance of others.

Effective delegation requires:

● objective analysis

● sound judgment

● firmness

● fairness

● sensitivity

Don't forget

Don't always delegate to the most obvious person – think about the longer-term development of your team.

Accountability

Individual accountability

Delegation means allocating responsibility for specific tasks to specific individuals and making them accountable for the results. Accountability is therefore at the heart of effective delegation. It needs to be clear and it needs to be monitored.

In the simplest form of delegated accountability, one named individual is given responsibility for completing the task. He or she is responsible and accountable for ensuring that the work is completed on time, to the required standard, and with whatever resources have been made available.

If the task is more complex, the manager may break it down into discrete elements and delegate accountability for each element to a different individual. In this case each element must be defined very precisely, so that there are no overlaps and everyone has a clear understanding of their responsibilities and of the results for which they are accountable.

Monitoring

However much you trust the individual whom you have made accountable for a specific task, you still need to keep an eye on progress. There are many options:

- personal report: you can ask the delegate to give you a one-to-one progress report at regular intervals

- written reports: you can ask for a written commentary at regular intervals, highlighting action taken, progress made, results achieved and any problems encountered

- summary emailed reports: you can ask for short, periodic progress reports

- ad hoc: you may prefer simply to call the delegate to your desk from time to time to give you an oral update

- open-door: you can rely on the delegate to give you an update on progress from time to time and to inform you of any problems that arise

- IT: you can arrange to be copied in electronically on key communications so that you can see how things are going

- meetings: you may want to set up a meeting not only with the individual accountable for the work but also with others involved

Each of the above methods has advantages and disadvantages.

For example, a written report can encourage the delegate to organize his or her thoughts and to provide a full account of progress; but it may also paint an overly-optimistic picture (perhaps showing the delegate in a flattering light) and skate over difficulties and potential problems.

An open door policy carries the dual risk of being either under-used, with the manager kept in the dark or insufficiently informed, or over-used, with the delegate becoming unduly reliant on input from the manager.

Choose whichever method, or combination of methods, suits you best and is most appropriate for the task in hand. You need to be able to:

- check progress and review what has been achieved so far

- satisfy yourself that the delegate is on course to deliver the desired result

- pinpoint problems and take any necessary remedial action

If the task is complex and of long duration, you may even want to consider using some of the project management tools described in Chapter 5, such as Gantt charts, milestones and performance criteria. Often, however, monitoring is best done systematically but with a light touch.

The benefits of effective monitoring are not always limited to the task in hand. It is not unusual that lessons learned from monitoring progress (or lack of progress) towards completing one task can be applied to other similar tasks or to other aspects of the work. These lessons may be either positive or negative. Experience in one area may have thrown up an elephant trap of some kind which could be waiting for you elsewhere, and which you should now be able to avoid. More positively, you may come across some approach that works spectacularly well and which you will now be able to use in other contexts.

Don't forget

Be prepared to learn something yourself from the way your delegate tackles the job.

Summary

- Failure to delegate means increased pressure and stress, and reduced personal effectiveness

- A manager who does not delegate effectively wastes time on low priority work and has insufficient time for the most important tasks

- The stimulus of new responsibilities can motivate staff and increase job satisfaction

- Delegation can give individuals the opportunity to learn new skills and to maximize their potential

- Effective delegation helps an organization to make optimum use of its human resources, thus enhancing its overall performance

- Both manager and delegate must be clear about the task to be carried out and the result expected, and it's usually best for this to be confirmed in writing

- The degree of delegated autonomy should be clearly defined

- Once the desired outcome is clearly understood, the delegate should be left to get on with it and to decide how that outcome is achieved

- The manager needs to give encouragement and support, particularly during the early stages

- Choose the best available person for the task: give careful consideration to the skills and experience needed, as well as to the importance and urgency of the task

- Accountability means giving responsibility for the task to one named individual

- Choose whichever method of monitoring suits you best and is most appropriate to the task

12 Managing Interviews

An interview can be almost as nerve-wracking for the interviewer as it is for the interviewee. Thorough preparation is the key.

Introduction

If you're a manager, recruiting a new member of your team is one of your most important tasks. Mistakes can be difficult to rectify and may have adverse long-term consequences both for you personally and for your organization.

An interview can help you to select the right person for the job, but it should be seen as just one element of the selection process. Not everyone who performs brilliantly at an interview performs brilliantly in the job.

Role Evaluation

The first, critical step is to think really hard about what you need. At this stage it can be useful to do some lateral thinking.

- Does the job need to be done in the same way that it's been done in the past?

- Do you want to take the opportunity to restructure your team, so that you can make better use of the available skills and experience – and of individual strengths?

- Do you need to bring together some tasks currently undertaken by different people?

- Or to separate out others, so that you can devote more resources to current priorities?

After all, neither the organization's goals nor your own priorities are set in stone. They may have to change to reflect changes in the external or internal environment, and managers are sometimes slow to make the consequential and necessary adjustments to their teams.

So begin by thinking through the role you'll want your new recruit to play.

- Are there any obvious gaps in the knowledge, skills and experience of your team?

- Or any less obvious attributes that would improve the job's value to the organization?

Careful evaluation of the new role is the first prerequisite for your interview preparation.

Job Description

Hot tip

Make sure the job description explains what results are expected.

Once you're clear about the new role, the next step is to prepare an accurate job description. The structure and precise content will vary according to the organization and the job, but it should normally include:

● Job title

● Reporting line

● Purpose

● Key objectives

● Main tasks

● Essential skills and experience needed

Accuracy and honesty are important. Do not shy away from mentioning aspects of the job that are either

● especially demanding

● especially boring

Any misleading information won't do anyone any favors. The job description needs to give potential applicants enough detail to enable them to form a considered judgment about their interest in the job and their suitability. So it should describe:

● the essential skills

● personal qualities needed

● specific detail about what the job-holder is expected to achieve

Sifting and Shortlisting

Minimum criteria

If the job is being advertised externally and you anticipate a large number of applications, it is essential to establish minimum criteria such as:

- educational or professional qualifications

- a specified amount of time spent in a similar job in order to screen out unsuitable applicants

Applications which satisfy the minimum criteria can then be considered, alongside other available evidence, in drawing up a short list of well qualified candidates for interview.

CVs and application forms

It's rare for an applicant to submit a CV which is factually inaccurate. But it may be a little economical with the truth:

- it may not tell the whole story or give a complete picture of the applicant's career

- it's not unknown for an applicant to exaggerate achievements, to claim personal credit for achievements that resulted from the combined efforts of a whole team

- it may omit negative factors.

So you need to read between the lines. It's worthwhile noting any gaps in the CV's chronology and any unsubstantiated claims: if the candidate is short-listed, these can be explored at interview.

A standard application form requiring candidates to answer the same set of questions can be useful: all applicants are put on the same footing, making it easier to compare candidates objectively against your criteria.

How many people you decide to short list for interview will depend upon

- quantity

- quality

of the applicants. Bear in mind that the longer your shortlist, the longer the interviewing process will take and the more difficult

Hot tip

Learn to read between the lines of a CV.

...cont'd

it may be (unless there is just one truly outstanding candidate) to come to a final decision. There is no hard and fast rule, but a maximum of six is often a good rule of thumb for the shortlist.

Other evidence

The CV and the application form will help you to reject unsuitable applicants and to home in on those who seem most suitable. But before finalizing your shortlist you should consider any other available evidence. This may include

- performance appraisals

- third-party accolades or relevant observations

- comments or personal recommendations from colleagues who have worked with the applicant

The weight you attach to this evidence will depend upon the reliability of the source. For example, a personal recommendation from a respected colleague whose judgment you trust and who knows the candidate well will carry a good deal of weight; positive comments from someone who knows the candidate less well and whose judgment is suspect, will carry much less weight.

The Interview

Structure

Sometimes, if you're a manager running a small team, you may conduct the interview on your own. At other times you may want or be required to involve others. In either case you need to consider in advance how to structure the interview. That will depend to some extent on what you see as its main purpose. For example, if it's abundantly clear that the candidate has all the technical qualifications and skills needed to do the job, you may want to concentrate on "softer" aspects, such as interpersonal skills, character and personality.

If, on the other hand, there are some really significant questions arising out of the candidate's CV, you may decide to structure the main part of the interview around those.

A common structure for an interview is:

1. An introductory "getting to know you" phase in which the candidate is set at ease, invited to talk about previous work and past experience, and asked why he or she is interested in the job.

2. A session focusing on the specific responsibilities of the job, filling in gaps in the candidate's CV and testing the extent of his or her relevant knowledge, skills and experience.

3. A phase aimed at exploring the candidate's personal qualities and character traits. This might include questions about wider interests or, in the case of senior jobs, questions about current affairs or social or economic issues which are aimed at assessing the candidate's breadth of vision, analytical ability and judgment.

4. Finally, the candidate should be given an opportunity to ask questions about the job or the organization – or to add anything to what he or she has said during the interview.

...cont'd

Interviewing panels quite commonly consist of three people. With a three-person panel

- the person chairing the interview should handle the first and last Steps

- one panel member from the part of the organization in which the selected candidate will work should cover Step 2

- someone from another part of the organization should cover Step 3

If there is an interviewing panel it's important for members to agree between them beforehand who will cover what. This avoids duplication and makes optimum use of each panel member.

Final Preparation

Your final preparation has two elements.

 Criteria

The first is to draw up a list of the criteria to be used in assessing candidates. Your starting point for this will probably be the role evaluation and job description, but you need to give your criteria careful thought and make sure they cover the key skills, experience and personal qualities you're looking for. You'll want to give more weight to some criteria than to others. Don't make your list of criteria too long (a maximum of six is often a good rule of thumb). This will complicate and lengthen the selection process. Focus on the essentials. If there is an interviewing panel you will need to brief the other members and share your list of criteria with them.

Hot tip

Think hard about what you'll need from the person you select.

 Check list

The second element of your final preparation is to arm yourself with a short check list of questions covering the key areas. Open questions (inviting more than a "yes" or "no" answer) are usually the most useful in encouraging the candidate to open up, to think and to talk. This should enable you to observe his or her communication skills and to obtain the information you need.

- "What?"

- "Why?"

- "How?"

are often the best words with which to begin your questions.

Do not, however, stick too rigidly to your check list. An interview should be a two-way exchange of information. It's best for each question to be built on the candidate's answer to the one before. The check list is simply a safety net to ensure that you cover all the essential ground.

Opening the interview

The opening of any interview is especially important. If, from the very beginning, there is a positive rapport between interviewer and interviewee and the candidate feels at ease, he or she will be more likely to open up and talk freely. This will help the interviewer to obtain the information that's needed to make well-informed judgments about the candidate's abilities and personality.

Most candidates will feel nervous to some degree, even if they do not show it. A welcoming greeting can make all the difference. So stand up, make eye contact, move towards the candidate, welcome him or her by name, and give a firm handshake. If there are others present, introduce them. Invite the candidate to sit down. Be courteous and considerate.

Listening and body language

Careful, concentrated listening is one of the interviewer's key skills. It's not as easy as you might think. Two common mistakes are to:

1. "switch off" when the interviewee says something that does not interest you

2. interrupt before he or she has completed what's being said

Don't forget

Prepare a check list of the essential points you need to cover.

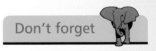

Don't forget

Begin the interview with an effective greeting.

...cont'd

Resist the temptation to interrupt, and make a real effort to focus on what is being said and to absorb the meaning.

It's important to show that you are listening attentively. You can do this by leaning forward slightly to show that you're interested, looking at the candidate with an open expression, and occasionally nodding to indicate agreement. It also helps if, from time to time, you summarize what is being said.

Do not talk too much. Ask each question as clearly and concisely as you can, and then wait and listen to the answer. A good rule of thumb is for the interviewer to speak for no more than 20 per cent of the time. In any interview the candidate should do most of the talking.

The interviewer should take care over his or her own body language – and pay careful attention to the interviewee's.

Don't forget

Listening is hard work – concentrate.

Beware

Don't talk too much yourself.

- Does the candidate's body language match – or contradict – what they are saying verbally?

- Watch the position of their body, arms and legs. Do these suggest confidence – or uncertainty and defensiveness?

- Pay particular attention to the eyes: these can be especially revealing. Does the candidate avert them, perhaps looking at the floor or the ceiling, at times when you would expect to have eye contact?

Don't forget

Watch for body language and eye contact.

Assessing Candidates

As soon as the candidate has left the room, make a few memory-jogging notes so that you will be able to distinguish one candidate from another when you come to review their performance.

You will probably have been able to jot down a few of the candidate's comments during the interview itself (especially if you are part of an interviewing panel), but now is the time to make a note of your overall impressions. These will be based on the candidate's demeanor and the way he or she speaks as well as on the content of what is said. If you are in doubt, trust your instincts.

One simple method of assessment is to prepare a sheet of paper with three columns.

- In the first, list each criterion.

- In the second column, alongside the criterion, allow space where you can make a brief note of any comments made during the interview or other evidence which illustrate the candidate's ability to meet, or failure to meet, that criterion.

- In the final, narrow, column you can enter your assessment of whether or not the candidate meets the criterion. This should take account not only of what has been said during the interview, but also of information derived from the CV, application form or any other source.

It's best not to over-complicate this. Three levels of assessment are usually sufficient:

- does not satisfy the criterion

- satisfies the criterion

- satisfies the criterion exceptionally well

In the happy event that you end up with more than one candidate who satisfies all the key criteria exceptionally well, be guided by your experience – and sheer gut instinct.

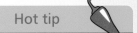

Hot tip

Assess whether each criterion is satisfied, not satisfied, or satisfied exceptionally well.

Hot tip

See Interview Assessment sheet on page 184.

Summary

- An interview is just one element of the selection process

- Begin with a careful evaluation of the role

- Prepare an accurate job description, and ensure that it makes clear what the job-holder is expected to achieve

- Establish minimum criteria to help you draw up a shortlist

- Consider all available evidence – CV, application form, performance appraisals, personal recommendations, etc

- A maximum of six is often a good rule of thumb in compiling a shortlist of people to be interviewed

- Plan the structure of the interview carefully

- Establish criteria to enable you to assess candidates

- Record your impressions immediately after the interviewee has left the room

- Prepare a check list of questions covering key areas, but don't stick to it too rigidly

- Take care over how you open the interview

- Pay attention to body language – both your own and the interviewee's

Resources

Career Development Check List

The following check list can be adapted according to your individual needs. It should be revisited periodically (at least once every six months) in order to check that you are on course to achieve your career development objectives.

1 How long do I want to be in my current job?

2 What results do I need to show by the time I move on?
- Key achievements
- New or enhanced experience
- New or enhanced skills
- Other

3 Where do I aim to be in five years time?

4 What action do I need to take now in order to get there?

5 Where do I aim to be in ten years' time?

6 Is there any action I need to take now in order to ensure that my longer career objective is achievable?

Simple "To Do" List

Description of Task	Priority	Result Needed	Deadline

Presentation Check List

1 What's the purpose?

2 Who are the audience?
- How many?
- Where from?
- How much experience? etc

3 What will the audience expect to get out of it?

4 What are my specific audience-based aims and objectives?

5 What's the setting like?
- Type and size of room
- Seating arrangements
- Equipment, etc

6 Method to be used (e.g. PowerPoint, Talk book, etc)

7 Length of presentation (normally 20 minutes maximum)

8 Key points to be included in the content

9 Anecdotes and examples to be used

10 How will I begin the presentation and draw the audience in?

11 How will I end the presentation?

Stakeholder Analysis

A simple two-axis diagram can provide a useful structure for prioritizing attention to relevant stakeholders. In identifying stakeholders, remember to include both internal and external ones.

The axes show "influence" and "interest": respectively, how much that individual or organization can affect what happens, and how much they are affected by what happens. Each stakeholder should be given a position somewhere on the diagram. If the diagram is put onto a flip chart, whiteboard or large sheet of paper where it can be preserved and accessed, stakeholders' positions can be moved over time to mimic the dynamism of reality, and new stakeholders can be added as necessary.

The diagram can be set up in the following way, with the vertical axis representing a scale from no influence at all to exceptional or over-riding influence, and the horizontal axis from no interest at all to exceptionally strong interest:

Don't forget

The amount of influence and/or interest which each stakeholder has may change over time.

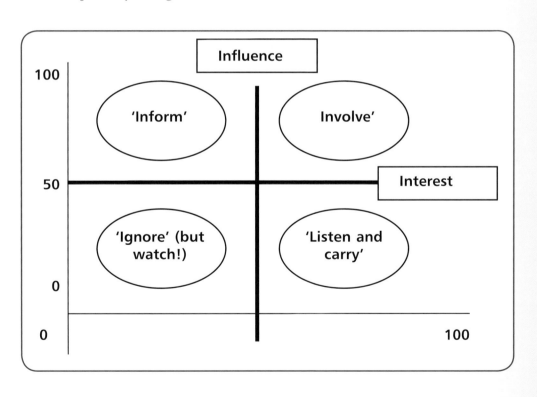

Risk Register

Every project carries some element of risk. It's important to identify the risks:

1 assess each one for probability and impact

2 consider possible countermeasures or contingency action

It's important that these are proportionate to the risk.

A risk register, reviewed and updated at regular intervals, is a useful way to record, assess and track risks:

Risk	Probability	Impact	Owner	Countermeasures	Status

Explanations

Risk: Brief description (or ID) of each risk (or obstacle) identified

Probability: Rank: VH (very high), H (high), M (medium), L (low), VL (very low)

Impact: Rank VH (very high), H (high), M (medium), L (low), VL (very low)

Owner: Name of the individual responsible for monitoring the risk and taking any necessary countermeasures

Countermeasures: Description of countermeasures or contingency action identified

Status: The current state of play

Risk Profile

A Risk Profile can provide an overall picture of risks and help to highlight those in respect of which countermeasures are most necessary.

For example, if five risks have been identified these could be numbered (1 to 5) and entered in the following table, with assessments for probability entered vertically and for impact horizontally:

Probability						
	Very high					
	High					
	Medium					
	Low					
	Very Low					
		Very Low	Low	Medium	High	Very High

Impact

Gantt Chart

	January	February	March	April	May
Activity A					
Activity B					
Activity C					
Activity D					
Activity E					

Appraisal Interview Check List

The following check list can be used to prepare for an interview appraising individual performance:

1 What evidence is there of performance during the past year? Identify tasks which have been accomplished

- exceptionally well and/or
- unsatisfactorily
- be specific and factual.

2 What factors can you identify that have affected performance (for good or bad)? Divide these into internal factors (i.e. within your own organization) and external factors

3 Identify new tasks and objectives for the forthcoming year, and put these in order of priority. Aim to reach agreement with the interviewee on a list of SMART objectives

4 Is there any training or other support that could help the interviewee to further improve performance in the job?

5 Is there anything you might suggest that would help the interviewee's longer-term career development?

Negotiation Check List

Purpose of negotiation
Ideal outcome
Fall back position
Bottom line
Key facts and figures
Killer arguments
Key individuals Supportive: Hostile: Uncertain:

Option Appraisal Check List

1. Identify options

2. List the pros and cons of each option

3. Establish criteria
   - cost
   - practicability
   - effectiveness
   - acceptability to stakeholders and staff
   - speed of implementation

4. Rank each criterion according to its importance (say on scale of 1 to 5)

5. Consider each option in turn and go through each criterion, awarding points (say from 0 to 10) according to the extent to which it satisfies that criterion

6. Multiply the points awarded by the weighting given to each criterion

7. Put the results into a table or onto a spreadsheet for ease of comparison

8. You can now see which option best meets your criteria

If there is very little to choose between your top options, don't be constrained by the arithmetic. Be guided by your experience and instinct.

EFQM Excellence Model

The European Foundation for Quality Management (EFQM) Excellence Model, used beyond the boundaries of Europe, is an assessment tool that allows an organization to be compared against best practice. It can be thought of as a large check list to help an organization identify its strengths and weaknesses in a systematic way.

The Model has nine criteria, some (enablers) relating to how an organization does things, and others (results) to what the organization achieves in quantified terms:

Enablers

1. Leadership

2. Policy and Strategy

3. People

4. Partnerships and Resources

5. Processes

Results

6. Customer Results

7. People Results

8. Society Results

9. Key Performance Results

The EFQM Excellence Model can be applied either to an organization as a whole or to individual units within an organization. It is most commonly used as a self-assessment tool, but some organizations have commissioned independent assessments based on the Model.

Balanced Scorecard

The Balanced Scorecard is a performance measurement, management and reporting framework that enables managers to look at the business from four key perspectives:

- The customer perspective – how do our customers see us?

- The internal business perspective – which processes and competencies do we need to excel at?

- Innovation and learning perspective – how can we continue to improve and excel?

- Financial perspective – how do we look to our financial stakeholders?

Within these four perspectives the organization decides on a series of objectives that are considered to be critical to success. Progress towards these objectives is then tackled through specific measures and targets, with specific initiatives being taken to deliver the improvements necessary to achieve the targets.

SWOT Analysis

SWOT analysis identifies Strengths, Weaknesses, Opportunities and Threats. It is a simple and versatile tool that can be used for organizations, parts of organizations or individuals.

Strengths and weaknesses refer to the present state. Opportunities and threats refer to the future.

Here are some examples of questions that might be asked when conducting a SWOT analysis:

Strengths

- What is done well?

- What are your advantages?

- What unique features or characteristics are in your favor?

- Consider such questions (a) from your own perspective and (b) from that of others.

- Be realistic but modest.

Weaknesses

- What is done badly?

- What are your disadvantages?

- What could be improved?

- What should be avoided?

Again, consider (a) from your own perspective and (b) from an external perspective – others may spot weaknesses that you do not.

Be realistic and face up to any unpleasant truths.

Opportunities

- What are the trends?

- Where might future opportunities arise?

Consider, for example, likely changes in:

- government policies

- economic developments

...cont'd

- market trends

- technology

- social or demographic patterns

Threats (include risks and obstacles)

What obstacles are there?

- How might these change in the future?

- How are others likely to react?

- Assess risks for probability and impact

Consider: prevention, reduction, contingency action or acceptance.

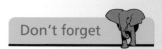

Strengths	Weaknesses
Opportunities	**Threats**

Interview Assessment Sheet

A simple method of assessment is to prepare, for each candidate, a sheet of paper with three columns, listing each of your selected criteria. Remember that you may want to give more weight to some criteria than to others.

Name of candidate:

Criterion	Evidence/comments/observations/ relevant factors	Assessment (NS/S/EWS)*

NS = Not satisfied

S = Satisfied

EWS = Exceptionally well satisfied

Further Reading

Business Coaching in easy steps *by Jon Poole*

Developing your Career in Management *by Jeremy G. Thorn*

Effective Project Management in easy steps *by John Carroll*

Embracing Change – Essential Steps to Make Your Future Today *by Tony Buzan*

Giving Great Presentations in easy steps *by Drew Provan*

How to be a Civil Servant *by Martin Stanley*

Leadership in easy steps *by Jon Poole*

Leading Change *by John P. Kotter*

Management Teams: Why They Succeed or Fail *by R. Meredith Belbin*

Public Speaking in easy steps *by Drew Provan*

Team Roles at Work *by R. Meredith Belbin*

The 7 Habits of Highly Effective People *by Stephen R. Covey*

The 80/20 Principle: The Secret of Achieving More with Less *by Richard Koch (Nicholas Brealey Publishing)*

The Effective Executive: The Definitive Guide to Getting the Right Things Done *by Peter F. Drucker*

The Essential Drucker: the Practice of Management *by Peter F. Drucker*

Who Are You? The Briggs Myers Personality Indicator and Personality Types *by Stuart Sloan*

Working with Emotional Intelligence *by Daniel Coleman*

For further information from the author, visit: www.tonyrossiter.co.uk.

Excerpt from Leadership in easy steps...

Being True to Yourself

In Chapter 1 we stressed the importance of being yourself rather than merely trying to mirror others' leadership styles. This sounds easy to do but does make the assumption you fully understand and appreciate who you are in the first instance.

Nature vs. nurture

Much is written on the subject of personality and, in particular, the 'nature vs. nurture' debate. That is, are you the person you are because of 'nature', i.e. the genetic coding that you were born with or due to 'nurture', i.e. the way you were brought up and the experiences that you have encountered and learnt from throughout the various stages in your life?

The answer is, you are who you are due to a complex combination of both nature and nurture and you should be proud of the resultant personality you have become. This is one of the main reasons why, in of becoming a leader, you should try to be yourself rather than trying to be someone else.

Look back to your childhood

Because your personality has gradually developed based on a combination of genetics and the experiences in your life, you'll probably be able to recall important moments in your life – especially from your childhood – where some of your early thinking, values and motivations started to take shape.

Think back to your childhood now and try to recall the types of games and activities that gave you the greatest satisfaction. Now try to relate these to work and the activities you enjoy the most.

You may notice that there are similarities in some of your favorite activities and the work you enjoy. We'll explore this some more later in this chapter.

Hot tip

Looking back at some of the games you played as a child can help you understand why you enjoy doing the things you do in your work life today.

to further develop your management skills

Be genuine

One of the critical elements of being an excellent leader is trust. You need to be able to have trust in those who work for you and with you. Most essentially, others must have trust in you – it cannot be a one way thing.

Trust is a fragile thing that can only be built over time but with the possibility of being lost in an instant following, perhaps, just one careless comment or act. The people who interact with you have learnt who you are and will be acutely aware of any changes in your behaviors and actions.

If you aren't genuine – attempting to be someone who you are not – they will be quick to see through your facade or act and will be immediately on guard.

Tell them what you're doing

If you have an open enough relationship with those who you work with, you should be able to make them aware that you are working on aspects of your leadership. Ask them for help by:

- Giving you feedback on any positive changes they notice

- Letting you know if any of the changes don't appear genuine

- Letting you know of changes they would like to see happen

- Hopefully supporting you and encouraging you – after all, these changes should ultimately benefit them!

Beware

You cannot expect others to trust you if you are not prepared to demonstrate a level of trust for them – it works two ways.

Behind Excellent Leaders

Behind every excellent leader... well, behind every one of us, in fact, is a highly complex and constantly changing mix of personality elements that make up 'you'. These include aspects such as:

- Your personality traits or predispositions

- Your personal values and beliefs

- Your behavioral strengths and weaknesses

- Your prime motivators or drivers

- Your knowledge and skills sets

- Your experience and capabilities

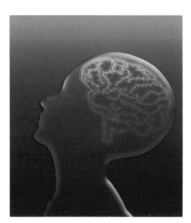

All of the above elements play an important role in helping to define the person you are and also your resulting leadership style.

Understanding yourself

Over the next few pages we will explore each of these elements in turn and the interrelationships between them. We will also help you understand their potential impact on your role as a leader and, most importantly, help you determine your own strengths and possible weaknesses relating to each element.

Only when you start to explore and understand these underlying elements of personality that drive the things you do, can you then be true to yourself and become a natural and genuine leader.

Exercises

From time to time, we will suggest exercises to help you discover more about yourself. You don't need to work through all of these. Feel free to dip in to those you think may help. In addition, in Chapter 10, you'll find references to a number of online resources where you can access more in-depth information and analyses relating to various aspects of your personality.

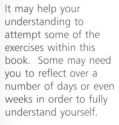

Don't forget

It may help your understanding to attempt some of the exercises within this book. Some may need you to reflect over a number of days or even weeks in order to fully understand yourself.

Index

W

T

U

V